WHO'S WHO — THE COBBLERS
The story of the players 1920-1988

FRONT COVER: The 1929-30 team.

WHO'S WHO —
THE COBBLERS

The story of the players
1920-1988

BY

FRANK GRANDE
assisted by
JOHN HARLEY

SPORTING & LEISURE PRESS
BUCKINGHAM, ENGLAND
MCMLXXXVIII

PUBLISHED BY SPORTING & LEISURE PRESS
BUCKINGHAM, ENGLAND
AND PRINTED BY
BURGESS & SON (ABINGDON) LIMITED
ABINGDON, ENGLAND

BOUND BY
CEDRIC CHIVERS LIMITED
BATH, ENGLAND

JACKET PRINTED BY
CHENEY & SONS LIMITED
BANBURY, OXON

PHOTOLITHOGRAPHY BY
CAMERA GRAPHIC LIMITED
AMERSHAM, ENGLAND

DISPLAY SET IN BASKERVILLE
AND TEXT SET IN 10/11pt BASKERVILLE BY
KEY COMPOSITION
NORTHAMPTON, ENGLAND

© Frank Grande 1988

ISBN 0 86023 427 4

CONTENTS

FOREWORD

by Derek Banks, Chairman of Northampton Town FC

In this, my fifth season as chairman of Northampton Town FC I can say, with hand on heart, that I have seen some very good football at the County Ground, played by some very good footballers.

Graham Carr has moulded together a young, enthusiastic, and exciting side in a short time; however, many of the older supporters enjoy nothing more than comparing them with the Cobblers of yesteryear.

Being a newcomer to the town, I am afraid that a lot of the names that are put forward are just that — names. Now I welcome this opportunity of having more of an insight into these men who have all worn the claret and white of this Football Club.

When Frank approached the Board for permission to write such a book I, together with my fellow directors, was all in favour of such a publication, knowing that his previous effort, a history of the Club, was well received by the supporters.

So I hope that the following pages inform the newer supporter of players past, remind the older supporters of days gone by, and make everyone a little more knowledgeable on Northampton Town FC.

We must all realise that, was it not for these stalwarts of the past, put down on paper together for the first time, by a man who we know as 'The Walking Encyclopaedia on the Cobblers', then we would not be able to watch this team challenging for greater things, this season.

INTRODUCTION

On completion of *The Cobblers*, one of the things that stood out was that, despite the amount of information it carried, it said little about the careers of the players, other than their moves to and from this club.

To correct this, the easiest way to cover the players is in the form of a Who's Who. By keeping it to statistics, this also allows the opportunity to put in as much information as possible.

However, rather than fill the whole book with statistics, these have been augmented by the memories of over 40 ex-players, ranging from some who were with us before the war, to those who were here just a few seasons ago. Some memories are happy, some sad, some funny, yet all the players hold an affection for the Club, a reflection on Northampton and its supporters.

The current players were correct at March 1988 but, by the time this is in print, there may well be changes, hence appearances and goals for these players have been omitted, as they are readily at hand in the Club programme.

Finally, the book updates the Club's history, and an exciting period as they make every effort to attain top-flight football.

Like the last book, this is written by a supporter for supporters, hoping that it helps the older supporter relive happy memories, and the younger one to have a better understanding of the players of yesteryear, who paraded in the claret and white of Northampton Town.

My thanks go to co-author John Harley, for his constant checking and rechecking of the facts and figures; Dave Walden, who once again allowed me to use his wonderful collection of photographs; *The Chronicle and Echo* who allowed me to use any of their photographs; to Peter Norton for the current crop of photographs; John Watson, who provided all the information on the 'Cricketing Cobblers'; to Northampton Town FC, and the Club's directors, for allowing me to go ahead with this project; to Ray Spiller and the Association of Football Statisticians of which I am proud to be a member, and the supporters of the Club, who have approached me continually over the last couple of years to ask 'When is the next one coming out?'; and last but not least, for the help and support of my family: my wife Tina, and my son Dusty.

KEY TO CAPTION CREDITS

PN   Pete Norton
G   E. Greenway
C&E   *Chronicle & Echo*

Cobbler's chairman, Derek Banks (2nd from right) discusses a point with
the Author (2nd from left) about the previous publication *The Cobblers*,
far left John Morris, now secretary of the British Boxing Board of
Control, and far right is Bob Church, Cobblers' Director and England
International Fisherman. (PN)

THE PLAYERS

Don Adams. (C&E)

If a player's full name is known it will be recorded; positions relate to the positions of the player's era, *ie:* a midfielder of today would be a wing half, or inside forward of the fifties. Unfortunately not all dates and places of birth, or of death, are known but what information I have has been recorded. Appearances are for League games, FA Cup games, League Cup, Divisional Cup and Freight Rover Trophy games; any other appearances (war games etc) will be recorded in the Notes. The Clubs for which each player has played are listed in chronological order, League clubs are followed by the years the player stayed there. The Notes record any interesting points, or records the player may have achieved in his career, and the career at Northampton records the month and date of joining and the month and date of leaving. (The players' pictures precede their entry.)

ADAMS, Donald F.   Centre forward
Bedford, 15.2.1931
23   7   (5.1951-5.1956)
Cobblers ('51-56), Bedford Town, Rushden Town.
County Youth player (1949). Father also played for the club in the early twenties.

Tony Adcock. (PN)

ADCOCK, Anthony Charles (Adi)

ADEY, Thomas William Wing half
Hetton le Hole 22.2.1901
11 — (6.1926-6.1927)
Bedlington, Hull City ('23-25), Swindon Town ('25-26), Northampton ('26-27), Durham ('27-28).

AITKEN, John Gordon Winger
Govan, Glasgow 17.9.1897 1.12.1967
9 5 (6.1927-5.1928)
Clyde, Third Lanark, Bury ('24), Southport ('24), Crewe ('25), Norwich ('26), Northampton ('27-28), Kilmarnock.

ALEXANDER, John E. Striker
Liverpool 3.10.1955
24 + 3 5 (6.1981-5.1982)
Ulysses, Millwall ('77-79), Reading ('79-81), Northampton ('81-82).

ALDRIDGE, Norman Full back
Walsall, 23.2.1921
2 — (6.1948-5.1949)
Foxford, West Bromwich Albion ('46-48), Northampton ('48-49), Headington, Locheed Leamington.

ALLAN, Charles E. Full back
Darlington c1910
15 — (5.1932-5.1934)
Darlington District, Northampton ('32-34), Darlington District.

ALLEN, Percy William Wing half
West Ham 2.7.1895 East Ham 21.10.1969
49 3 (7.1925-5.1927)
West Ham United ('19-23), Lincoln City ('23-25), Northampton ('26-28), Weymouth.

ALLEN, Ralph Slack Littlewood
Centre forward
Newborn on Tyne 30.6.1906 Blyth 9.5.1981
57 44 (10.1936-11.1938)
Dipton, Fulham ('28-31), Brentford ('31-34), Charlton ('34-36), Reading ('36-37), Northampton ('36-38), Torquay ('38-39).
Div 3 championship with Charlton, 1935. Still holds record number of goals for Charlton in a season, 32 in 1935. Joined Torquay in exchange for Haycock.

ALLEN, Robert A. Full back
Bromley 11.10.1916
5 — (2.1946-5.1947)
Orient ('33-34), Fulham ('34-37), Doncaster ('37-38), Brentford ('38-40), Northampton ('46-47), Colchester ('47-51), Bedford Town. Six war games for Northampton, also guested for Notts Forest during war. Captained Colchester into the League 1950, settled in Colchester.

ALLEN, Thomas Goalkeeper
Moxley, Staffs 1.5.1897
25 — (7.1933-5.1934)
Wednesday Bilston, Sunderland ('19-20), Southampton ('20-28), Coventry ('28-32), Accrington ('32-33), Northampton ('33-34).
Div 3 south championship with Southampton in 1922.

Thomas Allon.

ALLON, Thomas George Wing half
Blyth, Northumberland Sunderland
27.8.1899 4.1983
190 7 (1.1926-6.1932)
Coventry ('21-25), Nuneaton, Peterborough, Northampton ('26-32).
Cost Northampton £1,000 together with Maloney, from Peterborough.

AMBRIDGE, F.W. Goalkeeper
Wellingborough, c1900
17 —
Navy, Northampton ('21-22), Wellingborough.

ANDERSON, Gary Full back
Bow, 20.11.1955
16 — (3.1975-5.1976)
Tottenham Hotspurs ('72-75), Northampton ('75-76), Barking, Cheltenham, Billericay.

ANDERSON, John L. Inside forward
Glasgow, 5.4.1928
15 5 (6.1953-7.1954)
Partick Thistle, Northampton ('53-54), Exeter City ('54-55), Dundee, Wrexham ('56-59), Rochdale ('59-60), Chester ('60-61), Wrexham ('61-62).
Played in England, Scotland and Wales; trainer to Aldershot since 1980.

Jack Ansell. (C&E)

ANSELL, William (Jack)   Goalkeeper
Bletchley 4.8.1921
142   —   (3.1948-5.1952)
Bletchley Brickworks, Northampton ('48-52), Headington.
Suffered broken leg v Southend 1951; previously made 105 consecutive appearances. Still playing cricket in the early '80s.

Charles Anthony.

ANTHONY, Charles   Full back
Mansfield
84   —   (6.1929-5.1932)
Northampton ('29-32), Mansfield ('32-33).

ARMITAGE, John Henry   Centre half
Chapeltown, Leeds 21.8.1897.
4   —
Mexborough, Burnley ('24-26), Oldham ('26-29), Southend ('29-30), Northampton ('30-31), Halifax ('31-32).

ASHENDEN, Russell   Midfield
South Ockenden 4.2.1961
9 + 13   —   (2.1979-5.1980)
Northampton ('76-80), A.P. Leamington, Corby, Long Buckby.

ASHER, Sydney   Centre forward
Portsmouth 24.12.1930
22   11   (11.1956-5.1957)
Portsmouth ('48-50), Gloucester City, Hastings, Northampton ('56-57), Bedford Town, Skegness.
Signed on the strength of his performance for Hastings v Northampton.

ASHWORTH, Alec   Inside forward
Southport 1.10.1939
34   26   (. 1962-6.1963)
Everton ('58-60), Luton Town ('60-62), Northampton ('62-63), Preston North End ('63-65), Stockport ('65 loan), Altrincham.
Joined Luton from Everton as makeweight for Billy Bingham. Cobblers bought him after bid for Terry Bly failed; won an FA Cup runners-up medal with Preston in 1964, together with Div 3 championship medal with Cobblers in 1963.

AUSTIN, Terry   Centre forward
Isleworth 1.2.1954
49 + 1   13   (7.1983-5.1984)
Crystal Palace ('72-73), Ipswich ('73-76), Plymouth ('76-78), Walsall ('78-79), Mansfield ('79-80), Huddersfield ('80-82), Doncaster ('82-83), Northampton ('83-84), Stamford Town.
Was makeweight for Paul Mariner when he moved from Ipswich to Plymouth; set a record in 1979 by playing 49 league games for Walsall and Mansfield. Owns Insurance brokers in Mansfield.

BAILEY, Raymond   Centre half
St Neots 16.5.1944
1   —   (10.1971 loan)
Bedford Town, Gillingham ('60-71), Northampton (1971), Milton Keynes.
Last player to play for Cobblers and Northants Cricket Club. Right hand batsman and bowler, he also played for Bedfordshire and Buckinghamshire, managed Milton Keynes FC for a spell and is now a county ground groundsman.

BAINES, Stanley N.   Wing half/forward
Leicester 28.7.1920
1   —   (7.1946-7.1947)
Leicester City (war), Northampton ('46-47).
Played 2 games for Northampton during war, as guest.

BAKER, William Thomas   Goalkeeper
Shotton, Durham 17.8.1905
                    Shotton 30.3.1975
14   —   (7.1934-7.1935)
Crook Town, Southport ('29-32), Brentford ('32-34), Northampton ('34-35), Rochdale ('35-36).
Div 3 medal with Brentford 1933; before his death was greenkeeper with Shotton Golf Club.

Paul Bancroft. (PN)

BANCROFT, Paul   Midfield
Derby 10.9.1964
16 + 1   —   (7.1984-5.1985)
Derby County ('82-84), Crewe ('83 loan), Northampton ('84-85), Nuneaton Stafford Rangers, Kidderminster Harriers.
FA Trophy runners-up with Stafford 1987.

BANNISTER, James H.   Full back
Chesterfield 1.2.1929
25   —   (7.1958-8.1959)
Chesterfield ('50-52), Shrewsbury ('52-58), Northampton ('58-59), Aldershot ('59-61).

BARNES, Michael   Centre half
Reading 17.9.1963
25   1   (7.1984-5.1985)
Reading ('80-84), Northampton ('84-85).
Retired through injury.

BARON, Kevin   Inside forward
Preston 19.7.1926
27   4   (9.1958-5.1959)
Preston (war), Liverpool (war-'44), Southend ('54-58), Northampton ('58-59), Wisbech, Aldershot ('60-61), Maldon Town (Player/manager).
FA Cup runners-up medal Liverpool 1950.

BARRATT, Alfred G.   Centre half
Kettering 13.4.1920
1   —   (7.1938-9.1939)
Northampton ('38-40), Leicester ('47-49), Grimsby ('50-51), Southport ('51-52).
Also played one game for Northampton as war-time guest.

Roger Barron. (C&E)

BARRON, Roger W.   Goalkeeper
Northampton 30.4.1947
19   —   (7.1965-7.1969)
Northampton ('65-69), Bedford Town.
Son of Bill Barron.

Bill Barron. (C&E)

BARRON, William   Full back
Houghton le springs 26.10.1967
172   4   (12.1938-5.1951)
Wolverhampton Wanderers ('36-37), Charlton ('37-35), Northampton ('38-51), Kettering.
88 games and 19 goals for Northampton during war; also guested for Luton and Leicester, played for County Cricket Club, '46-51, left-handed bat, 181 appearances; highest score, 161 v Cambridge. Father of Roger.

BARTRAM, James L.   Forward
— c1911
14   6   (6.1935-12.1935)
Portsmouth ('30-31), North Shields, Falkirk,
Northampton ('35-36), Queen of the South.

BAXTER, Lawrence R.   Inside forward
Leicester 24.11.1931
17   2   (3.1952-11.1954)
Northampton ('52-54), Norwich ('54-55),
Gillingham ('55-57), Torquay ('57-62),
Cheltenham, Deal Town (Player/Manager).

BAXTER, William R.   Centre half
Edinburgh 23.4.1939
43   4   (6.1972-5.1973)
Broxburn Athletic, Ipswich ('60-71), Hull
City ('71-72), Watford ('71 loan),
Northampton ('72-73), Nuneaton.
Managed Northampton from October 1971.
Won two Div 2 and one Div 1 medals with
Ipswich.

BEAVON, David   Winger
Nottingham 8.12.1961
2   —   (3.1983-5.1983 loan)
Notts County ('79-81), Lincoln ('81-83),
Northampton ('83 loan), Kettering, Boston U.

BEDFORD, Sydney G. (Ginger)   Wing half
Northampton c1901
78   2   (7.1920-7.1924)
Northampton ('21-24), Brighton ('24-25),
Luton ('25-26), Rushden Town.

Frankie Belfon. (C&E)

BELFON, Frankie   Forward
Wellingborough 18.2.1965
78 + 17   18   (3.1983-5.1985)
Wellingborough, Northampton ('83-85),
Wellingborough, Buckingham Town,
Wellingborough.
County youth player with both
Wellingborough and Northampton.

BELL, Tom   Centre forward
Seaham Colliery 9.11.1906   Lincoln 2.7.1983
79   31   (12.1934-6.1936)
Dawdon Colliery, Torquay ('25-27), Merthyr
('27), Halifax Town ('27-30), Chesterfield
('30-32), Southport ('31-33), Luton Town
('33-34), Northampton ('34-38),
Wellingborough Town, Spalding.
Div 3 North championship with Chesterfield
1931. Last goal for Northampton was his
100th League goal.

BELLAMY, Ben Walter   Inside forward
Wollaston   Northampton
22.4.1891   20.12.1985
7   (cs1913-6.1921)
Northampton ('13-20), Kettering.
58 games and 11 goals for Northampton in
the Southern League; also played cricket for
Northamptonshire, '20-27; 353 appearances
as a wicket keeper and batsman; 652
dismissals; highest score 168 v Worcestershire.

Ian Benjamin. (PN)

BENJAMIN, Ian   Striker
Nottingham 11.12.1961
173 + 3   68   (8.1984-10.1987)
Sheffield United ('78-80), West Bromwich
Albion ('80-81), Notts County ('81-82),
Peterborough ('82-84), Northampton ('84-
87), Cambridge United ('87-), England Youth
International. Northampton's player-of-the-
year, 1987.

BENNETT, Jesse   Full back
Sheffield
65   —   (2.1934-6.1936)
Sheffield United ('27-32), Dronfield,
Coventry ('32-33), Northampton ('33-36).
Retired through injury.

BERRIDGE, T.E.   Wing half
Northampton
1   —   (10.1927-5.1928)
Northampton Nomads, Northampton ('27-
28).

Billy Best. (C&E)

BEST, William   Utility
Glasgow 7.9.1943
268 + 2   55   (7.1962-1.1968)
                      (9.1973-5.1977)
Pollock, Northampton ('62-68), Southend
('68-73), Northampton ('73-77), Bedford
Town, Corby Town.
Two spells with Northampton: captained the
side to promotion in 1977. Ex-player-of-the-
year; on retiring, became publican and ran a
decorating business with Graham Felton.

BILLINGHAM, Jack   Forward
Daventry 3.12.1914
3   —   (8.1935-8.1936)
Northampton ('35-36), Bristol City ('37-38),
Burnley ('38-49), Carlisle ('49-51), Southport
('51-55).
46 games and 32 goals for Northampton
during war, also guested for Darlington
during the war. Div 2 runners-up medal with
Burnley 1947. Returned to Daventry to work
with BBC.

BLENCOWE, Arthur George   Forward
Brackley 5.11.1916
2   —   (6.1937-6.1938)

Brackley Town, Northampton ('27-38),
Banbury.

Eddie Blunt. (G)

BLUNT, Edwin   Wing half
Tunstall 21.5.1918
98   5   (1.1938-war)
                   (war-7.1949)
Port Vale ('36-38), Northampton ('38-39),
Bury (war), Northampton ('46-49),
Accrington ('49-50).
19 games and one goal for Northampton
during war; also guested for Port Vale, Stoke,
Wrexham, Crewe, Bury, Charlton and Wolves
during war.

BOOK, Kim   Goalkeeper
Bath 12.2.1946
95   —   (10.1969-9.1971)
Bristol Rovers (a/m), Frome Town,
Bournemouth ('67-69), Northampton ('69-
71), Mansfield ('71 loan), Doncaster ('71-73),
Frome Town, Bath (a/m), Yeovil (a/m).
Brother of Manchester City player, Tony.
Saved penalty on his Bournemouth debut.

Percy Bosse. (G)

BOSSE, Percy Llewellyn   Wing half
Cardiff 18.10.1914
37   3   (9.1937-9.1939)
Cardiff   ('31-32),   Arsenal   ('32-37),
Northampton ('37-39).
Three appearances for Northampton during
war; set up a motor factors' in the town after
retiring.

Dave Bowen. (P.N)

BOWEN, David Llewellyn   Wing half
Masteg (Wales) 7.6.1928
35   1   (7.1947-7.1950)
                                     (7.1959-)
Northampton   ('47-50),   Arsenal   ('50-59),
Northampton ('59-60 as player).
Welsh International, 19 caps. Returned to
Northampton in 1959 as player manager for
£7,000, became Welsh part-time manager in
1964,   connected   with   Northampton   as
manager, general manager secretary and
director until 1986, took Northampton from
Div 4 to Div 1. Father of Keith.

Ted Bowen.

BOWEN, Edward C.   Centre forward
Darfield, Barnsley 1.7.1903
169   122   (2.1928-12.1931)

Wath. Arsenal ('25-27), Northampton ('27-
32), Bristol City ('32-34).
Scored hat-trick on his Northampton debut v
Norwich;   broke   goalscoring   record   at
Northampton that season with 34 goals.

BOWEN, Keith   Striker
Northampton 26.2.1958
71 + 5   25   (non contract)
Northampton ('76-81), Brentford ('81-83),
Colchester ('83-85), Northampton Spencer.
Welsh schoolboy and under-21 international.
County youth player '74-78. Leg injury in car
accident ended league career. Son of Dave.

BOWKER, Keith   Forward
West Bromwich 18.4.1951
4   —   (12.1976-1.1977 loan)
Birmingham   ('68-73),   Exeter   ('73-76),
Cambridge United ('76-77), Northampton
('77 loan), Torquay ('80).
Came to Northampton in exchange loan with
Jim Hall.

BOYD, M.S.   Winger
Local
2   (cs1926-7.1927)
Northampton ('26-27), Rushden Town.

BOYLE, Thomas W.   Forward
Sheffield 27.2.1897
153   35   (cs1930-5.1935)
Sheffield United ('21-29), Manchester United
('29-30), Northampton ('30-35), Scarborough
(player-manager).
FA Cup winners' medal with Sheffield United,
1925.

BRADFORD, Lowe   Forward
Scotland 1898
5   1   (3.1924-6.1924)
Clydehead, Dundee, Hibernians, Hartlepool
('22-23), Northampton ('24).

BRADSHAW, Harold   Winger
2   —   (7.1925-5.1926)
Northampton ('25).

BRADY, Paul   Defender
Birmingham 26.3.1961
64 + 2   3   (7.1981-3.1983)
Birmingham ('78-81), Northampton ('81-83),
Crewe ('83-85).
Retired through injury.

BRANSTON, Terence G.   Centre half
Rugby 25.7.1938

17

270 + 2   2   (10.1958-6.1967)
Northampton ('58-67), Luton Town ('67-72), Lincoln City ('72-74), Nuneaton, Enderby Town.
Granted a testimonial v Luton in 1987. Runs own driving school in Rugby.

Frank Brett.

BRETT, Frank   Full back
Kings Norton, 10.3.1899
271   4   (6.1923-6.1930)
Manchester United ('21), Redditch, Aston Villa ('22-23), Northampton ('23-29), Brighton ('30-35).
Became a coal merchant in Brighton.

BREWER, Anthony   Goalkeeper
Edmunton 20.5.1932
90   —   (12.1957-7.1961)
Millwall ('49-57), Northampton ('57-61), Bexley Heath, Rothwell Town.

BRIGHT, Gerald   Centre forward
Northampton 2.12.1934
4   —   (8.1957-5.1958)
Northampton ('56-58)

Jim Briscoe. (C&E)

BRISCOE, James   Winger
Clockface   Northampton
28.4.1917   17.4.1981
60   18   (9.1946-5.1949)
                                 as a player

Preston North End ('37-39), Hearts, Northampton ('46-59), Nuneaton (loan), Wolverton (Player manager).
Moved from Preston to Hearts, and Hearts to Northampton, together with Archie Garrett. Became 'colts' coach in 1949-53. Moved to Nuneaton for a loan spell in 1953 as part of the Frank Upton deal. During the war, guested for Arsenal, Crystal Palace, Blackburn, Brighton, Fulham, Millwall, and Southend.

BROADFOOT, Joseph   Winger
London 4.3.1960
18   1   (10.1965-5.1966)
Millwall ('58-63), Ipswich ('63-65), Northampton ('65-66), Millwall ('66-67), Ipswich ('67-68).

BRODIE, Charles T. (Chic)   Goalkeeper
Duntocher (Glasgow) 22.2.1937
97   —   (9.1961-10-1963)
Manchester City ('54-57), Gillingham ('57-58), Aldershot ('58-61), Wolves ('61), Northampton ('61-63), Brentford ('63-69), Margate.
Holds record of three consecutive League appearances, in three different Divisions, for three different Clubs: Aldershot (4), Wolves (1), and Northampton (3). 3rd Division championship medal with Northampton 1963. League career ended at Brentford, when dog ran on pitch and damaged ligaments in leg; became a London cabbie.

Eric Brookes. (C&E)

18

BROOKES, Eric   Full back
Staincross 3.2.1944
96 + 2   3   (7.1969-6.1971)
Manchester United (am), Barnsley ('61-69), Northampton ('69-71), Peterborough ('71-73), March Town, Ely Town, March Town (Player/manager), England schoolboy international, youth international, youngest player ever to play for Barnsley. Most FA Cup ties for Barnsley, 36. Father was groundsman at Oakwell.

BROOKS, John T.   Goalkeeper
London 23.8.1947
1   —   (10.1967-5.1968)
Queens Park Rangers ('66-67), Ipswich ('66-67), Northampton ('67-68), Guildford.

BROUGH, Neil   Midfield
Byfield, Northants 22.12.1965
7 + 7   —   (6.1984-5.1985)
Northampton ('84-85), Long Buckby.
County Youth cap with Northampton, 1982.

BROWN, Alfred   Wing half
Chadderton, Oldham 22.2.1909
62   1   (6.1933-2.1936)
Chamber Colliery, Oldham ('28-33), Northampton ('33-36), Mansfield ('36-38).

BROWN, Dennis (Bullets)   Inside forward
Reading 8.2.1944
43 + 5   11   (2.1967-7.1969)
Cheltenham, Chelsea ('62-64), Swindon ('64-66), Northampton ('66-69), Aldershot ('69-74), Margate, Barnet, Cheltenham.
Joined Northampton in exchange deal with Bobby Jones; lost a kneecap in a car accident in 1967.

Laurie Brown.

BROWN, Laurie   Centre forward/half
Shildon 22.8.1937
38   25   (10.1960-8.1961)
Bishop Auckland, Darlington ('58), Bishop Auckland, Northampton ('60-61), Arsenal ('61-63), Tottenham ('63-65), Norwich ('66-68), Bradford ('68-69) Player/Manager, Altrincham (Player Manager), Kings Lynn (Player Manager).
England Amateur international. Record fee £30,000 for Northampton when he joined Arsenal. Now tanker driver in Durham.

Bobby Brown. (C&E)

BROWN, R.   Winger
Scotland c1911
90   27   (cs1934-6.1936)
Morton, Queens Park Rangers ('32-34), Northampton ('34-36), Notts Forest ('36-39).

BROWN, Robert H.   Centre forward
Streatham 2.5.1940
55   24   (12.1963-10.1966)
Barnet, Fulham ('60-61), Watford ('61-63), Northampton ('63-66), Cardiff ('66-68).
England Amateur International. Scored both Barnet's goals in the 1959 Amateur Cup final. Became Welsh team coach, and Hull Youth team coach.

BROWN, Stephen   Midfield
Northampton 6.7.1966
14 +   3   (6.1984-6.1985)
Northampton ('84-85)

BROWN, W. Y.   Centre forward
South Inch
2   —   —
Queens Park Rangers ('11-12), Chelsea ('12-13), Bristol City ('13-15), Swansea ('20-22), Portsmouth ('22), Northampton ('22-23).

Bill Brown. (C&E)

John Buchanan.

BROWN, William D. F.   Goalkeeper
Arbroath 8.10.1931
21   —   (10.1966-2.1967)
Dundee, Tottenham ('59-66), Northampton
('66-67), Hamilton Steelers (Canada).
28 Scottish caps; one 'B' cap, member of Spurs
League and Cup double side, moved into real
estate in Canada, returned to Britain in a
similar capacity.

BRUCK, Dietmar J.   Midfield/defender
Danzig (Germany) 19.4.1944
45   —   (6.1972-6.1974)
Coventry ('62-70), Charlton ('70-72),
Northampton ('72-74), Nuneaton. Managed
Weymouth, Redditch and Coventry Sporting.

BRYANT, Steve P.   Defender
Islington 5.9.1953
115+2   5   (12.1967-3.1982)
                              (3.1979-5.1982)
Birmingham ('71-76), Sheffield Wednesday
('76), Northampton ('76-78), Portsmouth ('78-
82), Northampton ('82).
Emigrated to Australia.

BUCHANAN, David   Striker
Newcastle 23.6.1962
3+1   —   (10.1982-11.1983 loan)
Leicester ('79-83), Northampton ('83),
Peterborough ('83-84), Blyth Spartans,
Sunderland ('86-87), York City ('87 loan).

BUCHANAN, John   Midfield
Dingwell 19.9.1951
193+13   36   (11.1970-10.1974)
                              (10.1981-5.1983)
Ross County, Northampton ('70-75), Cardiff
('75-81), Northampton ('81-83), Wolverton,
Ross County.
Joined Cardiff in exchange deal with John
Farrington; returned to Northampton as
player coach.

BUCK, Anthony   Striker
Oxford 18.8.1944
Seaford, Oxford ('62-67), Newport ('67-68),
Rochdale ('68-72), Bradford City ('71),
Northampton ('72-74), Bedford Town.

BUCKBY, Leonard C.   Centre half
Northants
4   —   (6.1926-6.1927)
Northampton ('26-27), Wellingborough
Town.

BUKOWSKI, Dave   Defender
Newcastle 2.11.1952
10+3   —   (11.1971-5.1973)
Northampton ('71-73), Blyth Spartans.

BUNCE, Paul

BURN, Ralph G.   Forward
Ainwick 9.11.1931
1   —   (8.1950-7.1954)
Northampton ('50-54), Crewe ('54-55),
Rushden Town.

BURNARD, Walter Thomas   Inside forward
Northampton 4.10.1894
26   5   (cs1920-6.1922)
Northampton ('20-22), Rushden Town.

BURROWS, Adrian M.   Centre half
Sutton 16.1.1959
105   5   (7.1982-6.1984)

20

Mansfield ('79-82), Northampton ('82-84), Plymouth ('84-), Southend ('87 loan).

BURT, James H.   Full back
Harthill 5.4.1950
17+5   —   (7.1972-6.1973)
Whitburn, Leicester ('67-70), Aldershot ('70-72), Northampton ('72-73), Rochdale ('73-74).

BUSHELL, Mark   Defender
Northampton 5.6.1968
1   —   Non contract
Northampton ('85-87), Corby Town

BYATT, Dennis   Defender
Hillingdon 8.8.1958
51+4   3   (6.1979-2.1981)
Fulham ('76-78), Peterborough ('78-79), Northampton ('79-81), Wealdstone. Won FA Trophy and Gola League championship with Wealdstone.

BYRNE, Johnny   Midfield
Newton, Glasgow 20.5.1939
42   4   (12.1967-2.1969)
Pollock, Preston North End ('58-59), Queen of the South, Tranmere ('60-61), Hibernians, Barnsley ('62-64), Peterborough ('64-67), Northampton ('67-68).

CAINE, Brian   Goalkeeper
Nelson 20.6.1936
1   —   (7.1961-10.1961)
Burnley ('54-56 amateur), Accrington ('56-57 amateur), Blackpool ('57-59), Coventry ('59-61), Northampton ('61), Barrow ('61-65).
Whilst at Coventry played under the name 'Mr X' as a guest. In his first 7 seasons made only 3 appearances. One of the shortest stays at Northampton.

Maurice Candlin. (C&E)

CANDLIN, Maurice H.   Defender
Jarrow on Tyne 11.11.1921
151   2   (2.1949-7.1957)
Yoker Athletic, Clydebank, Partick Thistle, Northampton ('49-53), Shrewsbury ('46-49), Wellingborough (player manager).
Took player manager's job at Wellingborough 12 months after retiring from the game. Later took a public house and a newsagents, before retiring to Carlisle.

CANNING, Lawrence   Wing half
Cowdenbeath 1.11.1925
2   —   (6.1956-6.1957)
Paget Rangers, Aston Villa ('52-54), Kettering, Northampton ('56-57), Nuneaton. Now works for BBC as a sports commentator.

CARLTON, David G.   Midfield
London, 2.11.1952
188+6   7   (10.1973-10.1976)
                            (9.1980-7.1982)
Fulham ('70-73), Northampton ('73-77), Brentford ('77-80), Northampton ('80-82).
Retired in 1982 to take up a sports business.

Graham Carr. (PN)

CARR, Graham W.   Centre half
Newcastle 25.10.1944
91+1   —   (8.1962-6.1968)
Northampton ('62-68), York City ('68-69), Bradford ('69-70), Altrincham, Telford, Weymouth.
England Youth International. Captain of Telford when they won the FA Trophy. Manager of Weymouth, Poole, Nuneaton and Northampton. Won Southern League Championship (Nuneaton), Fourth Division Championship (Northampton).

CARSON, Alec   Wing half
Clarkson, Renfrewshire 12.11.1942
8   —   (11.1959-5.1963)
Northampton ('59-63), Aldershot ('63-64), Cheltenham, Worcester, Hereford.

Bill Cave.

CAVE, William   Goalkeeper
Northampton c1907
105   —   (cs1926-7.1937)
Northampton ('26-37)

Phil Cavener. (PN)

CAVENER, Philip   Winger
Tynemouth 2.6.1961
49+5   5   (7.1984-2.1986)
Burnley ('80-82), Bradford City ('82-83), Gillingham ('83-84), Northampton ('84-86), Peterborough ('86), Southend ('86), Kettering ('86-).
Set up a health gym in Sandy. Badly injured in road crash, tail end of the '86/87 season.

CHAMBERS, Len   Winger
Northampton
28   1   (Amateur)
Rushden, Northampton ('20-22), Rushden.

CHAPMAN, W.   Wing half
Rothwell
9   —   (9.1924-2.1925)
Rothwell, Northampton ('24-25), Rothwell.

Phil Chard. (PN)

CHARD, Phillip John

Lew Chatterley.

22

CHATTERLEY, Lewis Defender
Birmingham 15.2.1945
27   2   (9.1971-2.1972)
Aston Villa ('62-71), Doncaster ('70 loan), Northampton ('71-72), Grimsby ('72-74), Southampton ('74-76), Torquay ('76-78).
England Youth International. Player coach at Torquay, returned to Southampton as coach, moved to Sunderland as number 2; 1988, took charge of Poole Town.

CHERRY, James Forward
Wigan
10   2   (7.1933-7.1934)
Prescott Cables, Wigan Borough, Northampton ('33-34), Walsall ('34-35).

CHRISTIE, Derrick Winger
Bletchley 15.3.1957
130 + 25   21   (3.1975-10.1978)
Northampton ('74-78), Cambridge United ('78-84), Reading ('84-85), Cardiff ('85-86), Peterborough ('86-87), Corby.
Made more appearances as a substitute for Northampton than any other player.

CHURCHMAN, E. Forward
—
2   1   (cs1919-6.1921)
Northampton ('20-21).
Also made two Southern League appearances.

CIEGELSKI, Wayne Centre half
Bedwelty 11.1.1956
11   —   (3.1975-5.1975 loan)
Tottenham ('73-75), Northampton ('75), Schlake 04, Wrexham ('77-82), Port Vale ('84-86).
Welsh Under 21 international.

CIVIL, H. Wing half
Northampton
2   —   (cs1922-cs1923)
Northampton ('22-23).

CLAPTON, Dennis Forward
London 12.10.1939
1   —   (9.1961-9.1962)
Arsenal ('58-61), Northampton ('61-62), Orient ('62-63).
England Youth International, brother of England International, Danny.

John Clarke. (C&E)

CLARKE, John Defender
Northampton 23.10.1946
255 + 6   1   (7.1965-12.1975)
Northampton ('65-76)
County youth cap '62-65; England Youth International 1965. Retired through injury 1975; granted testimonial v Leicester 1976.

CLAYPOLE, Anthony Full back
Weldon 13.2.1937
125   1   (3.1954-10.1962)
Northampton ('56-62), Cheltenham, Corby, Wellingborough.
League career ended with broken leg in 1961, three weeks after he wed; became a car salesman and later took a hotel in Cornwall.

John Clifford. (G)

CLIFFORD, John Charles Goalkeeper
Newport 24.9.1906   Newport 22.6.1961
14   —   (11.1938-9.1939)
Crystal Palace ('28-33), Blackburn ('33-38), Northampton ('38-39).
Guested for Bournemouth and Brighton during the war.

COCHRANE, Alexander Fraser (Sandy)   Inside forward
Glasgow 8.8.1903
52   8   (2.1934-5.1935)
Shawfield, Alloa, Middlesbrough ('29-30), Darlington ('30-31).
Bradford City ('31-32), Chesterfield ('32), Llannelly ('32-33), Northampton ('33-35), Swindon ('35-36).

COCKBURN, G. W.   Winger
Gateshead, c1907
1   —   (cs1926-6.1927)
Gateshead district, Northampton ('26-27).

Vic Cockcroft. (C&E)

COCKCROFT, Victor   Full back
Harbourne 25.2.1941
52 + 1   1   (7.1962-6.1967)
Wolves ('59-62), Northampton ('62-67), Rochdale ('67-68), Kidderminster Harriers. England Youth International. Northampton's first used substitute; coach to Kidderminster.

COCKLE, Ernest S.   Centre forward
East Ham 12.9.1896   11.6.1966
104   47
Maidstone, Arsenal ('22-23), Luton Town ('23-24), Northampton ('24-28), Wigan Boro' ('28-30).

Norman Coe. (C&E)

COE, Norman C.   Goalkeeper
Pentrechynth 6.12.1940
62   —   (7.1960-5.1966)
Arsenal ('58-59), Gravesend, Northampton ('60-66), Kings Lynn.

Peter Coffill. (C&E)

COFFILL, Peter   Midfield
Romford 14.2.1957
75 + 7   5   (8.1981-6.1983)
Watford ('75-78), Torquay ('78-81), Northampton ('81-83), Aylesbury, Wellingborough, Aylesbury, Billericay, Chelmsford.

COLEMAN, Geoff   Full back
Bedworth 13.5.1936
18   —   (5.1955-6.1959)
Bedworth, Northampton ('55-58). Managed Bedworth and Nuneaton.

Bill Coley. (C&E)

COLEY, William E.   Wing half
Wolverhampton 17.9.1916
112   7   (7.1947-5.1951)
Wolves ('36-38), Bournemouth ('38-46), Torquay ('46-47), Northampton ('47-51), Exeter ('51-52).

Made 51 appearances and scored one goal for Club, as wartime guest. First Cobblers player to be sent off after the war; fined £2. Reserve team coach 1953-55; took a hotel on the south coast.

Ben Collins. (C&E)

Bob Corbett. (C&E)

COLLINS, Ben V.   Defender
Kislingbury 9.3.1928
224   —   (3.1948-5.1960)
Northampton ('48-60).
Owner of sports shop in Northampton.

CONNELL, Peter   Full back
East Kilbride 26.11.1927
13   —   (5.1951-5.1953)
Morton, Northampton ('51-53)

COOK, Colin   Centre forward
North Shields 8.1.1909
12   3   (6.1936-6.1938)
South Shields, North Shields, Crook Town, Chesterfield ('32-34), Luton ('34-36), Northampton ('36-38).

COOK, John   Inside forward
Sunderland 27.7.1897
19   2   (7.1924-6.1925)
Middlesbrough ('15-20), Notts County ('20-24), Northampton ('24-25).

COOKE, Barry   Wing half
Wolverhampton 22.1.1935
64   2   (7.1959-5.1962)
Erdington, West Bromwich Albion ('55-59), Northampton ('59-62).
England Youth International.

COOKE, Peter C.   Utility
Northampton 15.1.1962
4 + 1   1   (7.1980-6.1981)
Northampton ('78-81).
County youth player 1979-80.

CORBETT, Robert   Full back
Newburn 16.3.1922
8   1   (8.1957-7.1958)
Throckley Wharf, Newcastle ('46-54), Middlesbrough ('54-57), Northampton ('57-58).
1951 FA Runners-up medal with Newcastle, later managed Brierly Hill.

CORDICE, Neil   Striker
Amersham 7.4.1960
4 + 4   1   (7.1978-5.1979)
Fleckwell Heath, Wycombe Youth, Tooting and Mitcham, Northampton ('78-79), Wealdstone.
FA Trophy finalist, represented FAXI. Brother to Alan, of the England semi-professional XI.

COTTERILL W. A.   Forward
Local
1   —   (7.1937-6.1938)
Northampton ('37-38).

COWEN, James E.   Forward
Heningham c1907   1950
2   1   (7.1927-5.1928)
Whitehaven, Nelson, Barnoldswick, Northampton ('27-29), Southport ('29-30), Aldershot ('30-31), Peterborough.
Returned to electrical engineer's job in Middlesbrough.

COY, Robert

CRAVEN, Joseph   Left back
Glasgow c1912
3   —   (1.1936-5.1936)
Parkhead, Partick Thistle, St Mirren, Northampton ('35-36), Accrington ('36-37).

CRAWFORD, G. W.   Defender
Sunderland
2   —   (6.1930-5.1931)

CRILLY, Thomas — Full back
Stockton-on-Tees — Derby
20.7.1895 — 18.1.1960
59 — 1 — (6.1933-5.1935)
Stockton, Hartlepool ('20-24), Derby County ('24-28), Crystal Palace ('28-33), Northampton ('33-35), Scunthorpe ('35) player/manager.
38-years-old when he made his debut; first two moves were together with his best friend, W. Thom.

CROSS, Jack — Centre forward
Durham, 5.2.1927
12 — 9 — (10.1953-1.1954)
Guildford City, Bournemouth ('47-53), Northampton ('53), Sheffield United ('53-55), Reading ('55).
Spent only three months at Northampton, moved to Sheffield United for double the fee they paid Bournemouth; holds a BA.

John Croy. (C&E)

CROY, John — Centre half
Falkirk 23.2.1925 — Northampton c1980
26 — — — (7.1950-6.1965)
Third Lanark, Northampton ('50-55), Corby, Wellingborough.

J. Cuff. (G)

CUFF, J. — Winger
Lancashire
1 — — — (8.1938-5.1939)
Everton ('36-38), Northampton ('38-39).

Paul Culpin. (PN)

CULPIN, Paul

CURTIS, L. H. — Forward
Yorkshire
2 — 1 — (7.1938-6.1939)
Barnsley (amateur), Army, Northampton ('38-39).

CURTIS, Paul — Full back
London 1.7.1963
32 — 1 — (7.1985-10.1986)
Charlton ('81-85), Northampton ('85-86), Corby, Kettering.
Now employed locally as estate agent sales negotiator.

DALY, Joseph — Winger
Lancaster 28.12.1899
37 — 7 — (7.1927-6.1928)
Cliftonville, Notts County ('23-28), Northampton ('27-28), Luton ('28-30).

DANKS, Derek — Inside forward
Stoke, 15.2.1931
1 — — — (11.1953-6.1955)
Northampton ('53-55), Corby.

DAVIDS, Neil — Central defender
Bingley 22.9.1955
9 — — — (9.1975-10.1975 loan)
Leeds ('72-73), Norwich ('73-76), Northampton ('75) loan, Stockport ('76) loan, Swansea ('76-78), Wigan ('78-80),

Bromsgrove.
England Youth International; sent off while on loan to Cobblers.

DAVIE, James G.   Wing half
Newton (Scotland) 7.9.1922
76   1   (7.1950-7.1953)
Bridgetown Victoria, Newton Victoria, Kilmarnock, Preston North End ('48-50), Northampton ('50-53), Shrewsbury.

A. T. Davies.

DAVIES, Arthur Thomas   Winger
Nelson
12   1   Amateur
Nelson, Cambridge University, Corinthians. England Amateur International; Cambridge blue; schoolteacher at Northampton Grammar School.

DAVIES, Frank Palmer   Wing half
Swansea 1.8.1903   Northampton 1.1.70
158   6   (8.1930-6.1934)
Swansea (amateur), Charlton ('27-28), Portsmouth ('28-30), Northampton ('30-34), Nantwich ('30-34).

L. Davies.

DAVIES, L .
Welsh International, coach to Cobblers first-ever League side.

DAVIES, Oliver   Wing half
St Albans
1   —   (Amateur)
St Albans, Northampton ('33-34).

Albert Dawes.

DAWES, Albert George   Forward
Aldershot   Goring on Sea
23.4.1907   23.6.1973
174   93   (cs1929-12.1923)
Frimley Green, Northampton ('29-33), Crystal Palace ('33-36), Luton ('36-38), Crystal Palace ('38-39), Aldershot ('39-40).

England trialist 1935, represented South v North 1937. Guested for Crystal Palace, Reading and Arsenal during war; middle order batsman for Northants 1933; one appearance.

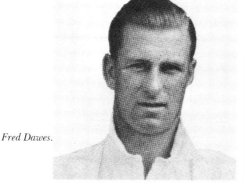

Fred Dawes.

Bob Dennison. (C&E)

DAWES, Fredrick   Full back
Frimley Green 2.5.1911
225   5   (cs1929-2.1936)
Frimley Green, Northampton ('29-36),

DAWES, Ian   Central defender
Aldershot 8.1.1965
4 + 2   —   (7.1985-3.1986)
Newcastle ('83-85), Northampton ('85-86). England Schoolboy International.

DAWSON, William   Centre forward
Glasgow 5.2.1931
14   7   (3.1955-6.1956)
Glasgow Ashfield, Northampton ('54-56).

DEACON, Richard   Forward
Glasgow 1910
4   1   (10.1935-3.1936)
Wolves ('29-31), West Ham United ('31-34), Chelsea ('34-35), Glenavon ('35-36), Northampton ('35-36), Lincoln ('36-39). Guested for Darlington during war.

DEAKIN, Michael R. E.   Centre forward
Birmingham 25.10.1933
48   31   (10.1959-2.1961)
Bromsgrove, Crystal Palace ('54-59), Northampton ('54-58), Aldershot ('61-62), Nuneaton.
Brother of Villa's Alan Deakin. Joined Northampton in exchange deal with Alan Woan; ironically both players played together at Aldershot.

DENNISON, Robert Smith   Centre half
Ambleside 6.3.1912
32   —   (1.1945-5.1948 as a player)
Reddcliff, Newcastle ('29-34), Notts Forest ('34-35), Fulham ('35-39), Northampton ('45-48).
Came from a family of 10, the only Englishman, the rest all Scots!
Started as an inside forward, guested for Fulham during the war; also 191 games and one goal for Northampton during war. Took over as Colts coach 1948. Became Northampton manager 1949-1955, then managed Middlesbrough, Hereford and Coventry.

Peter Denyer. (C&E)

DENYER, Peter   Midfield/defender
Haslemere 26.11.1957
159 + 10   35   (7.1979-5.1983)

Chiddingford Wanderers, Portsmouth ('75-79), Northampton ('79-83), Kettering ('83-85), Nuneaton, Blacktown (Australia), Boston.
Wore every outfield shirt for Northampton. Was assistant team manager and promotions manager at Kettering, now living in Australia.

W. A. Dickinson. (G)

DICKINSON, W. A.   Inside forward
Lancashire c1915
22   6   (10.1937-9.1939)
Everton ('34-37), Northampton ('37-39).

Arthur Dixon. (C&E)

DIXON, Arthur   Inside forward
Middleton 17.11.1921
77   26   (11.1979-10.1951)
Ailieston Juniors, Queens Park, Clyde, Hearts, Northampton ('49-52), Leicester C. ('52-53), Kettering.
Son of the former Hearts trainer, was selected to represent Scotland v the RAF, until it was discovered he was an Englishman.

DIXON, Cecil H.   Winger
Trowbridge 28.3.1935
16   4   (8.1961-5.1962)
Cardiff ('54-57), Newport C. ('57-61), Northampton ('61-62).
Later emigrated to Australia.

DOCHERTY, James   Forward
Clydebank 24.1.1925
1   —   (7.1950-3.1951)
Renfrew Juniors, Myrtle Greenock, Celtic, Northampton ('50-51), Stirling Albion.

DODGIN, Norman   Wing half
Gateshead 1.11.1921
19   1   (9.1951-4.1953)
Gateshead BC, Whitehall BC, Newcastle ('46-49), Reading ('49-51), Northampton ('51-53), Exeter ('53-58) (Player manager).
Managed Exeter, Oldham, Yeovil and Barrow. Uncle of Cobblers' manager of '70s, Bill Dodgin.

Warren Donald. (PN)

DONALD, Warren (Wazzer)

Glenville Donegal. (PN)

DONEGAL, Glenville

DOWSEY, John   Wing half
Gateshead, -.5.1905   Costolk 27.10.1942
95   7   (11.1931-5.1934)
Hunwick Villa, Newcastle ('24-26), West Ham
United ('26-27), Carlisle ('27-28), Sunderland
('28-29), Notts County ('29-31), Northampton
('31-34).
Div 3s championship with Notts County 1931.

DRAPER, Richard W.   Centre forward
Leamington 26.9.1932
52   22   (6.1955-6.1957)
West Bromwich Albion ('50-52), Lockheed
Leamington,   Northampton   ('55-57),
Kettering, Rugby.
Stayed part-time throughout his career.

Ted Duckhouse. (C&E)

DUCKHOUSE, Edward   Centre half
Walsall 9.4.1918
71   —   (8.1950-6.1952)
West Bromwich Albion ('36-38), Streetley
Works, Shefford; Birmingham ('47-50),
Northampton ('50-52), Rushden.

DUNKLEY, Maurice E.   Outside right
Kettering 19.2.1914
31   5   (8.1936-3.1938)
                         (7.1949-7.1950)
Kettering, Northampton ('36-38), Manchester
City ('38-46), Kettering, Northampton ('49-
50), Corby.
Moved to Manchester City in exchange for
three players; a middle order batsman for
Northants '37-39, highest score 70 v
Yorkshire. Guested for Manchester City,
Leicester, Walsall, West Brom, West Ham,
Millwall and Northampton during the war. 49
games, nine goals during war, for
Northampton.

DUTTON, Charles A.   Centre forward
Rugeley, Staffs 10.4.1934
10   2   (3.1956-12.1957)
Derby City ('51-53), Coventry ('53-55),
Northampton   ('55-57),   Lockheed
Leamington.

Keith East. (C&E)

EAST, Keith M. G.   Forward
Southampton 31.10.1944
32 + 3   9   (6.1970-5.1971)
Portsmouth ('61-63), Swindon ('63-66),
Stockport ('66-68), Bournemouth ('68-70),
Northampton ('70-71), Crewe ('71-72), South
Africa, Corinthian Casuals.
While at Stockport, scored a goal 6 seconds
from kick-off.

ECCLES, Joseph   Winger
Stoke on Trent
15   1   (cs1938-5.1929)
Wolsley Motors, Aston Villa ('24-26), West
Ham ('26-28), Northampton ('28-29),
Coventry ('29-31).

EDELSTON, Maurice   Inside forward
Hull, 27.4.1918   Tilchip 1975
44   17   (7.1952-5.1953)
Fulham ('36-38) (amateur), Brentford ('38-
45), Reading ('45-52), Northampton ('52-54).
England Amateur International, England
Victory International, appeared for Great
Britain Olympic team 1936, while still a

schoolboy. His father was manager of Reading when he signed; guested for Aldershot, Arsenal, Brentford and Liverpool during war, represented the FA v RAF in 1946. Scored within 10 seconds of Cobblers' debut v Exeter. A schoolteacher by profession. Joined BBC as commentator.

EDWARDS, Evan J.   Winger
Merthyr 14.12.1898
11   2   (cs1926-6.1927)
Merthyr T. ('20-23), Wolves ('23-25), Northampton ('26-27), Darlington ('27-29), Clapton ('29-30).

EDWARDS, Robert Henry   Centre forward
Guildford 22.5.1931
23   10   (3.1961-5.1962)
Chelsea ('51-55), Swindon ('55-58), Norwich ('58-60), Northampton ('60-62), Kings Lynn.

EDWARDS, Sydney Charles   Wing half
Northampton 16.8.1912
7   1   (cs1934-3.1936)
Northampton ('34-36), Rushden Town, Kettering Town.

Reg Elvy. (C&E)

ELVY, Reginald   Goalkeeper
Leeds 25.11.1920
72   —   (7.1956-7.1959)
Halifax (war-'47), Bolton ('47-51), Blackburn ('51-56), Northampton ('56-59).

Bob Ellwood. (G)

ELLWOOD, Robert J.   Forward
Worcester c1919
27   3   (8.1938-9.1939)
Fulham (amateur), Tunbridge Wells, Worcester City, Northampton ('38-39).
10 wartime appearances.

Jack English. (C&E)

ENGLISH, Jack — Outside right
Durham — Northampton
19.3.1923 — 18.11.1985
322 — 143 — (10.1946-6.1960)
Northampton Town ('46-60), Rugby Town. Guested for Bristol City during war, son of ex-Northampton manager. Div 3 south top scorer '52-53. Most goals in a career for Northampton, 143; scored on every Div 3 south ground, won an award in *Sporting Life* for his goalscoring prowess; only two goals off the record for most goals from the wing ('33) — in 1954.

ETHERIDGE, Brian — Inside forward
Northampton 4.3.1944
21 — 1 — (7.1963-2.1966)
Northampton ('61-66), Brentford ('66-68), Royal Darling, Corby Town, Wellingborough. England Youth International and County youth player ('60-62).

EVANS, Charles J. — Wing half
Cardiff 31.1.1897
17 — 2 — (12.1924-6.1925)
Cardiff ('22-24), Northampton ('24-25), Grimsby ('25-26).

Mike Everitt. (C&E)

EVERITT, Michael — Utility
Clacton 16.1.1941
225 + 1 — 17 — (2.1961-3.1967)
Arsenal ('58-61), Northampton ('61-67), Plymouth ('67-68), Brighton ('68-69), Plymouth City (player/manager).
Div 3 championship with Northampton 1963. After Plymouth City, took up managerial posts with Wimbledon, Brentford, coach at Leicester. Ran an Arabian contractors' team in Middle East; now scout at Notts County.

Fred Eyre.

EYRE, Fred M. B. — Inside forward
Northampton 29.9.1903
1 — — — (7.1930-5.1931)
Wolverton, Northampton ('30-31), Rushden Town.

FACER, Albert — Defender
— 15.7.1901
2 — — — (7.1922-7.1924)
Northampton ('22-24), Higham Town. Now lives in retirement at Hardingstone.

Bernard Fagan. (C&E)

FAGAN, Bernard — Midfield
Houghton le spring 29.1.1949
8 — — — (7.1969-5.1970)
Sunderland ('67-69), Northampton ('69-70), Scarborough Town.
FA Vase finalist with Scarborough.

John Fairbrother. (C&E)

FAIRBROTHER, John   Forward
Cricklewood 12.2.1941
158+6   61   (2.1968-9.1971)
Bennetts End, Watford ('59-62), Worcester,
Peterborough ('65-68), Northampton ('68-
71), Mansfield ('71-73), Torquay ('73-74),
Bath City, Barnet.

Ray Fairfax. (C&E)

FAIRFAX, Raymond G.   (7.1968-6.1971)
Smethwick 13.1.1941
138   2   (7.1968-6.1971)
West Bromwich Albion ('59-68),
Northampton ('68-71), Wellingborough,
Olney Town (player/manager).
Became WBA commercial manager 1974,
assistant secretary 1976; Port Vale secretary
1985.

FAIRHURST, William Shaw   Full back
New Dalaval 1.1.1902   Blyth 2.1.1979
13   —   (6.1932-5.1933)
Middlesbrough ('27-28), Southport ('28-29),
Nelson ('29-32), Northampton, ('32-33),
Hartlepool, ('34-35), Tranmere ('35-36).

FARMER, Kevin   Defender/attacker)
Ramsgate 24.1.1960
78+9   12   (8.1979-5.1982)
Leicester City ('77-79), Northampton ('79-81),
Bedworth.
Retired from League football due to injury.

FARR, Fredrick   Wing half
Bristol
2   —   (7.1935-5.1936)
Bath, Northampton ('35-36).

FARRINGTON, John R.   Winger/midfield
Lynmouth 19.6.1947
241+11   31   (10.1974-5.1979)
Wolves ('65-69), Leicester ('69-73), Cardiff
('73-74), Northampton ('74-79), Leamington
(player/manager).
Joined Cobblers in exchange deal with John
Buchanan, to Cardiff.

FAULKES, Brian   Full back
Abingdon, 10.4.1945
52   2   (7.1967-7.1969)
Abingdon, Reading ('65-67), Northampton
('67-69), Torquay ('69-70), Bath, Abingdon.

'Sonny' Feehan. (C&E)

FEEHAN, Ignatious (Sonny)   Goalkeeper
Dublin 17.9.1926
40   —   (8.1950-6.1952)
Bohemians (amateur), Waterford,
Manchester United ('48-50), Northampton
('50-54), Brentford ('54-56).
Now connected with Cogenhoe WMC.

Graham Felton. (C&E)

FELTON, Graham   Winger
Cambridge 1.3.1949
269 + 15   27
Cambridge United, Northampton ('66-76),
Barnsley ('76-77), Kettering, Bedford,
Wellingborough.
England Youth International, now runs
painting and decorating business with Billy
Best.

FERRARI, Fredrick Joseph   Wing half
Stratford, 22.5.1901   Sheffield 6.8.1970
18   —   (10.1925-5.1926)
Leyton ('21-25), Northampton ('25-26),
Sheffield Wednesday ('26-28), Norwich ('28-
29), Barrow ('29-30), Nelson ('30-31).

FISHER, Peter   Wing half
Edinburgh 17.2.1920
8   —   (9.1947-8.1950)
Northampton ('47-48), Shrewsbury ('48-50),
Wrexham ('50-51), Bedford.

Ron Flowers.

FLOWERS, Ronald   Wing half
Edlington 28.7.1934
63 + 1   4   (9.1967-6.1969)
Wolves ('51-67), Northampton ('67-69),
Telford (player/coach).
49 England Caps, three League championship
medals with Wolves, one FA Cup winners'
medal with Wolves (1960); member of
England's 1966 World Cup squad. Came to
Northampton as player/coach, took over as
player/manager in 1968. Won the FA Trophy
with Telford. Later ran a sports shop in
Wolverhampton.

Bob Folds. (C&E)

FOLDS, Robert J.   Full back
Bedford 18.4.1949
31   —   (8.1971-5.1972)
Gillingham ('67-71), Northampton ('71-72),
Bedford, Hitchin, Wellingborough,
Buckingham.

Theo Foley. (C&E)

FOLEY, Theodore C.   Full back
Dublin 2.4.1937

220   11   (5.1961-6.1967)
Home Farm, Burnley ('54-55), Exeter City
('55-61), Northampton ('61-67), Charlton
('67-68).
Eire International 9 caps. 100% penalty
record at Northampton; Club captain from
1963. Became Charlton's manager, then
coaching jobs with Millwall (twice), QPR and,
at present, Arsenal.

FORBES, Frederick James   Winger
Leith, 5.8.1894
35   3   (6.1932-6.1933)
Hearts, Everton ('20-23), Plymouth ('23-26),
Bristol Rovers ('26-31), Leith, Northampton
('32-33), Airdrie.

FORREST, C.   Wing half
Shildon
2   —   (8.1922-5.1923)
Shildon, Clapton Orient ('20-22),
Northampton ('22-23), Spennymoor.

FORSTER, Martyn   Full back
Corby, 1.2.1963
48 + 1   —   (7.1983-6.1984)
Kettering, Northampton ('83-84), Corby.
County youth player with Kettering ('79-81).

FOTHERINGHAM, James   Centre half
Hamilton 19.12.1933   Corby 1977
12   —   (8.1959-5.1960)
Arsenal   ('52-57),   Hearts   ('57-59),
Northampton ('59-61).
County Youth player with Corby Boys' Club.
Scottish 'B' International. National coach to
the Libyan team.

Tommy Fowler. (C&E)

FOWLER, Thomas   Outside left
Prescott 16.12.1924
552   89   (4.1945-12.1961)
St   Helens   Boys,   Everton   ('39-45),
Northampton ('45-61), Aldershot ('61-63).
More appearances for Northampton than any
other player. Wounded while on active service
in Normandy. Playing career spanned 18
seasons at Northampton; scored two hat-tricks
in his career, 10 years apart. Works at a local
factory.

FRASER, William C.   Inside forward
Blyth c1907
3   1   (10.1933-5.1934)
Southampton   ('27-30),   Fulham   ('30-33),
Northampton ('33-34).

FRASER, William C. C.   Inside forward
Stirling
20   4   (11.1926-5.1928)
Stirling   District,   Northampton   ('27-28),
Aldershot ('28).

Edward Freeman.

FREEMAN, Edward (Neddy)   Winger
Northampton   Northampton
-.7.1887   7.12.1945
48   4   (cs1906-5.1921)
Stoke City ('04-06), Northampton ('06-21).
319 Southern League games, and 70 goals.
County cricketer; right hand bat, medium
pace bowler, 16 appearances, between 1908-
1920.

FREEMAN, Neil   Goalkeeper
Northampton 16.2.1955
30   —   (8.1982-2.1983)
Arsenal ('72-74), Grimsby ('74-76), Northampton ('75 loan), Southend ('76-78), Birmingham ('78-80), Walsall ('80 loan), Huddersfield ('81 loan), Peterborough ('80), Northampton ('82-83).
Did not appear in his first spell, sent off on his league debut, later joined the police.

Neville Freeman. (C&E)

FREEMAN, Neville   Goalkeeper
Pitsford 25.1.1925   Northampton 1984
1   —   (10.1949-5.1951)
Northampton ('49-51), Wellingborough.

FREIMANIS, Edward   Forward
Latvia 22.2.1920
19   4   (8.1948-5.1950)
Peterborough, Northampton ('48-50), Nuneaton, Latvian International.

FRENCH, Jim R.   Inside forward
Stockton 27.1.1926
1   —   (8.1951-5.1953)
Middlesbrough (war-'59), Southend ('49-51), Northampton ('51-53), Darlington ('53-55).
Moved from Middlesbrough to Southend with brother John.

FRIAR, Paul   Full back
Glasgow 6.6.1963
16   —   (3.1986-5.1986 loan)
Leicester ('80-83), Rotherham ('83-84), Motherwell ('84-85), Charlton ('85-86), Northampton ('86 loan), Aldershot ('86-87).

FROGGATT, John L.   Centre forward
Ashton under Lyme 13.12.1945
43   13   (9.1978-6.1979)
East Kirby, Notts County ('66-68), Ilkeston, Boston United, Colchester ('74-76), Port Vale ('76-78), Northampton ('78-79), Boston United.
Later manager of Boston.

FROST, Stanley D.   Outside right
Northampton 19.10.1922
6   1   (1.1947-5.1948)
Northampton (war), Leicester ('45-47), Northampton ('47), Rugby Town, one war game for Northampton.

Wakeley Gage. (C&E)

GAGE, Wakeley   Centre half
Northampton 5.5.1958
248+4   22   (10-1979-8.1985)
Desborough Town, Northampton ('79-85), Chester ('85), Peterborough ('85-86), Crewe ('86-).
Northampton's 'player of the year' three times.

Colin Gale. (C&E)

GALE, Colin M.   Centre half
Pontypridd 31.8.1932
222   2   (3.1956-8.1956)
Cardiff ('50-56), Northampton ('56-61),
Wisbech.

GARNER, Tim   Goalkeeper
Hem 30.3.1961
2   —   (4.1986 N.C.)
Nuneaton, Kidderminster, Northampton
('86), Corby.

GARNHAM, Stuart E.   Goalkeeper
Selby 30.11.1955
13   —   (9.1974-10.1974 loan)
                           (8.1977-10.1977 loan)
Wolves ('73-76), Northampton ('74 loan),
Peterborough ('76-78), Northampton ('77
loan).
Only player to have two loan spells at
Northampton.

Archie Garrett. (C&E)

GARRETT, Archibald   Centre forward
Lesmahagow 17.6.1919
99   56   (9.1946-12.1947)
                           (12.1948-5.1951)
Preston North End ('37-39), Hearts,
Northampton ('46-47), Birmingham ('47-48),
Northampton ('48-51), Wisbech, Holbeach.
During the war made 13 appearances and
scored 9 goals for Northampton. Moved from
Preston to Hearts and onto Northampton
together with Jim Briscoe. Joined
Birmingham for £10,000.

GARVEY, James
Paisley, Lanarkshire 4.6.1919
1   —   (7.1939-9.1939)
Corby, Northampton ('39), Leicester ('45).

Tony Geidmintis. (C&E)

GEIDMENTIS, Anthony   Full back
London 30.7.1949
69   1   (2.1978-7.1979)
Workington ('66-76), Watford ('76-77),
Northampton ('77-79), Halifax ('79-80).
Made debut for Workington aged 15.
Suffered heart attack while playing for
Halifax, causing him to quit the game.

GEORGE, Herbert Stewart   Winger
Wellingborough -.4.1905
24   4   (cs1924-5.1926)
Wellingborough, Irchester, Northampton
('24-25), Rushden, Bedford.

GERNON, Irvine   Full back
Birmingham 30.12.1962
14   —   (10.1986-1.1987)
Ipswich ('78-87), Newcastle ('85 loan),
Northampton ('86 loan), Gillingham ('86-).

Dave Gilbert. (PN)

GILBERT, David James

GILLESPIE, Pat   Defender
Belishill 5.7.1928
1   —   (8.1947-11.1947)
Partick Thistle, Watford (war-'47),
Northampton ('47), Doncaster ('47-48).

GILLIGAN, Ian   Midfield
Abingdon 2.5.1957
4   1   (1.1977-2.1977)
Swindon ('74-77), Northampton ('76 loan),
Huddersfield ('77 loan), Trowbridge.

Peter Gleasure. (PN)

GLEASURE, Peter Francis

GORMAN, Keith   Striker
Bishop Auckland 13.10.1966
— +2   —   (12.1986-1.1987 loan)
Ipswich ('84-87), Colchester ('85 loan),
Northampton ('86 loan), Darlington ('87-).

Bill Gormlie. (G)

GORMLIE, William Joseph   Goalkeeper
Liverpool -.4.1911   Belgium -.7.1976
148   —   (6.1935-9.1939)
Fleetwood, Wimer Villa, Blackburn ('31-35),
Northampton ('35-39), Lincoln ('39).
Later manager of Anderlecht, Osled and
racing club Jetta; also coached the Belgian
national team.

Trevor Gould. (C&E)

GOULD, Trevor   Midfield/defender
Coventry 5.3.1950
105+3   6   (10.1970-6.1973)
Coventry ('67-70), Northampton ('70-73),
Bedford (player/manager), Rushden,
Aylesbury (player/manager).
England Youth International. Brother of
Bobby Gould. Now manager of Aylesbury.

GRAHAM, William   Forward
Preston
48   10   (2.1922-5.1924)
Lancaster, Northampton ('22-24), Wrexham
('24-25).

GRAY, George R.   Wing half
Sunderland
12   —   (12.1923-6.1924)
West Hartlepool, Swansea ('19-21), Bury ('21-
23), Northampton ('23-24), Durham ('24-25).

John Gregory.

GREGORY, John C.   Midfield/defender
Scunthorpe 11.5.1954
202   10   (1.1973-6.1977)
Northampton ('73-77), Aston Villa ('77-79),
Brighton ('79-81), QPR ('81-86), Derby ('86-).
Six full England caps.

Frank Grendon.

GRENDON, Frank Joseph W.   Wing half
Farnham 5.9.1891   Northampton -.3.1984
43   —   (9.1914-6.1922)
Northampton ('14-22), Rushden.
52 games for Northampton in the Southern
League.

GRIFFIN, Frank   Outside right
Manchester 28.3.1928
17   —   (7.1959-6.1960)
St Augustine's, Bolton ('44-48 amateur),
Eccles, Shrewsbury ('49-50), West Bromwich
Albion ('50-59), Northampton ('59-60),
Wellington, Sankeys, Worthon United
(manager).
Scored winning goal for WBA in the 1953 FA
Cup final. Dave Bowen's first signing as
manager.

GROOME,
  Joseph Phoenix George   Centre forward
Apsley, Herts   Beckenham
1.9.1901   20.8.1956
13   6   (Amateur)
Apsley Town, Northampton ('26-27),
Watford ('27-28), QPR ('28-29).

Ken Gunn. (G)

GUNN, Kenneth   Full back
Dunfermline
79   1   (6.1937-6.1939)
Newmains, Swansea ('32-35), Port Vale ('35-
37), Northampton ('37-39).
Ran a coalmerchants business in
Northampton.

GUNNELL, Richard Chas   Winger
Harpenden, Herts   Harpenden
10.4.1899   23.5.1977
13   1   (8.1926-5.1927)
Hertford, Northampton ('26-27), Bedford.

HAILS, William   Outside right
Nettlesworth 19.2.1935
63   13   (11.1962-6.1964)
Lincoln ('53-54), Peterborough ('54-62),
Northampton ('62-64), Luton ('64-65).
Division three championship with
Northampton ('63); moved to Luton in
exchange for Harry Walden, later
Peterborough, after three years as coach.
Moved on to Watford as physio.

Jim Hall. (C&E)

HALL, James   Centre forward
Northampton 2.3.1945
135 + 2   37   (7.1963-12.1967)
                              (3.1975-6.1978)
Northampton ('63-67), Peterborough ('67-75), Northampton ('75-78), Cambridge United ('76 loan), Cambridge City ('76-77).
England Youth International. Moved to Peterborough in exchange deal with John Byrne; 4th Division championship medal with Peterborough. Most goals in a career for Peterborough 137. Helped three clubs out of the fourth division. Player of the Year for Northampton (1976). Can be heard on Hospital radio giving commentary on Northampton's games.

HAMMILL, Stuart   Winger
Glasgow 22.1.1960
4   2   (3.1986-6.1986
                              non contract)
Leicester ('80-82), Scunthorpe ('82-83), Pollock, Nuneaton, Kettering, Northampton ('85-86), Finland, Altrincham, Scarborough ('87-).

Len Hammond.

HAMMOND, Leonard   Goalkeeper
Rugby 12.9.1901   Rugby 24.6.1983
326   —   (9.1924-7.1933)
North Western United, Rugby Town, Northampton ('24-33), Notts County ('33-35), Nuneaton, Rugby Town.
More games as a goalkeeper than any other player.

HARRINGTON, J.   Winger
Hendesford
8   —   (6.1928-6.1929)
Wolves ('26-28), Northampton ('28-29).

HARRIS, Alan

Joe Harron.

HARRON, Joseph   Winger
Langley Park, Durham 19.3.1900   19.2.1961
21   1   (7.1921-3.1922)
Hull City ('19-21), Northampton ('21-22), York ('22-24), Sheffield Wednesday ('24-25), York ('25-27), Scarborough, Barnsley ('30), Dartford.

Bryan Harvey. (C&E)

HARVEY, Bryan R.   Goalkeeper
London 26.8.1938
181   —   (10.1963-5.1968)
March Town, Wisbech, Newcastle ('58-61),

Cambridge United ('61-62), New Yorkers, Blackpool ('62-63), Northampton ('63-68), Kettering, Plymouth City.
Saved seven penalties in the 1964/65 season.

HASKINS, Anthony   Full back
Northampton 26.7.1935
8   —   (10.1959-11.1962)
Northampton ('59-62), Cheltenham, Kings Lynn.
Connected with local football and cricket for some years; also became a class I referee. Son of local boxer.

HATTON, Robert J.   Centre forward
Kingston on Hull 10.4.1947
32 + 4   8   (10.1968-7.1969)
Wolves   ('64-67),   Bolton   ('67-68),
Northampton ('68-69), Carlisle ('69-71),
Birmingham ('71-76), Blackpool ('76-78),
Luton ('78-80), Sheffield United ('80-82),
Cardiff ('83-84).

Barry Hawkings. (C&E)

HAWKINGS, Barry   Centre forward
Birmingham 7.11.1931
69   27   (6.1957-5.1959)
Coventry   ('49-56),   Lincoln   ('56-57),
Northampton ('57-59), Gravesend, Wisbech.

Peter Hawkins. (C&E)

HAWKINS, Peter M.   Forward
Swansea 18.12.1951
52 + 9   10   (12.1968-11.1973)
Northampton ('68-73), Bedford, Weymouth, Yeovil.
Welsh schoolboy international. Youngest player to play for Northampton at the time (16 years 351 days); was once a sub v Scunthorpe, while his brother sat on the other subs' bench.

Len Hawtin.

HAWTIN, Leonard Charles   Full back
Northampton 2.7.1892
13   —   (Amateur)
Northampton ('20-23).

Joe Haycox. (G)

41

HAYCOX, Joseph   Centre forward
—
20   6   (11.1938-6.1939)
Cheltenham, Newport ('32-34), Bristol City ('34-36), Torquay ('36-38), Northampton ('38-39).

HAYES, Austin W. P.   Forward
London 15.7.1958   London 2.12.1986
74 + 4   14   (7.1983-5.1985)
Southampton ('76-81), Millwall ('81-83), Northampton ('83-85), Barnet, Finland.
Eire International (one cap). Once had a reserve game at Southampton cancelled, when he jumped onto the cross bar, and broke it! Died at the age of 28, from lung cancer.

Ray Haywood. (C&E)

HAYWOOD, Ray   Forward
Dudley 12.1.1949
14 + 2   2   (3.1977-10.1977)
Stourbridge, Shrewsbury ('70-77), Northampton ('77), Kidderminster.

HAZELDINE, Donald   Inside forward
Arnold 10.7.1929
23   4   (6.1954-5.1955)
Notts Regent, Derby County ('51-54), Northampton ('54-55), Boston.
Joined Northampton as makeweight in the Frank Upton deal. Member of the Boston team that beat Derby 6-0 in FA cup.

HEASELGRAVE, Samuel   Inside forward
Smethwick   Birmingham
1.10.1916   22.4.1975
47   5   (10.1945-6.1948)
Bearward Swifts, Warley Lions, Brierly Hill Alliance, WBA ('38-45), Northampton ('45-48), Boston.

11 games and four goals for Northampton during the war, also guest for Walsall. All England Bowls champion 1963. Became a solicitor in Bearward.

Mark Heeley. (PN)

HEELEY, Mark D.   Winger/midfield
Peterborough 8.9.1959
99 + 8   6   (3.1980-6.1983)
Peterborough ('76-77), Arsenal ('77-80), Northampton ('80-83), Aylesbury, Buckingham, Peterborough ('85), Rushden, Buckingham.
Highest fee paid by Northampton at the time £33,000; turned part-time in 1982.

HENRY, Charlie   Utility
Acton, 13.2.1962
4   1   (3.1987-4.1987)
Swindon ('81-), Northampton ('87 loan).
Played for the Division four champions two seasons running: Swindon in 1986, Northampton 1987.

HENSON, George Horace   Inside forward
Stony Stratford 25.12.1911
52   18   (10.1932-11.1934)
Wolverton, Northampton ('32,34), Wolves ('34-36), Swansea ('36-37), Bradford ('37-38), Sheffield United ('38-39).

HESLOP, Brian   Defender/midfield
Carlisle 4.8.1947
53 + 1   —   (2.1971-6.1972)
Carlisle ('65-67), Sunderland ('67-71), Northampton ('71-72), Workington ('72-77).
Brother of George Heslop, late of Manchester City.

Bob Hewison.

HEWISON, Robert   Wing half
Backworth Newcastle   Bristol
25.3.1889   -4.1964
106   9   (6.1920-4.1925)
East Hollywell Villa, Whitley Athletic,
Newcastle ('08-15), Leeds ('15-19), Newcastle
('19-20), Northampton ('20-25, player/
manager).
Became Leeds City secretary while they were
wound up, as he was recovering from a
broken leg. Northampton's player/manager
from 1920-25; joined them for £250, later
managed QPR, Bristol City, Guildford, Bath
and was Bristol Rovers scout.

John Hewitt. (G)

HEWITT, John Joseph   Wing half
Hamsterley, Durham 15.6.1911
64   12   (10.1935-6.1939)
Evenwood, Everton ('30), Hartlepool ('30-31),
Norwich ('31-35), Northampton ('36-39),
Southport ('39).

HEWITT, Edwin   Wing half
—
1   —   (7.1936-5.1937)
Aston Villa (Jnr), Northampton ('36-37).

HICKS, Tom George   Full back
Trehaford, Wales
5   —   (cs1928-6.1929)
Pontypridd, Preston North End ('26-27),
Notts Forest ('27-28), Northampton ('28-29).

HIGGINS, Tom   Wing half
Glasgow
3   —   (9.1934-5.1935)
Hearts, Northampton ('34-35), Scunthorpe.

HILL, David   Goalkeeper
Kettering 28.9.1953
1   —   (apprentice)
Northampton ('69-73).

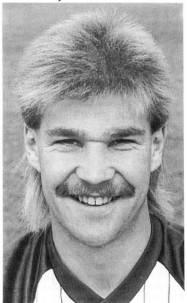

Richard Hill. (PN)

HILL, Richard   Midfield
Hinckley 20.9.1963
105   52   (6.1985-4.1987)
Leicester ('80-82), Nuneaton, Northampton
('85-87), Watford ('87), Oxford ('87),
Northampton's record transfer: £265,000 to
Watford.

HINSON, Ronald Henry   Forward
Chelveston 9.10.1915
10   4   (9.1933-5.1936)
Rushden, Northampton ('33-34), Irchester (loan), Northampton ('34-36), Rushden.

HOBBS, Ernest C.   Inside forward
Wellingborough
1   —   (8.1923-5.1924)
Wellingborough, Northampton ('23-24), Exeter ('24-25), Tunbridge Wells, Exeter ('26-27).

John Hold. (C&E)

HOLD, John D.   Forward
Southampton 28.3.1948
43 + 2   10   (9.1971-3.1973)
Fareham Town, Portsmouth (Jnr), Bournemouth ('64-71), Crewe ('71 loan), Northampton ('71-73), Weymouth, Gosport. Now working as area manager for supermarket chain.

HOLT, David   Forward
Northampton
1   —   (7.1936-7.1937)

HOLTON, Clifford   Forward
Oxford 29.4.1929
66   53   (9.1961-12.1962)
Oxford City, Arsenal ('47-58), Watford ('58-61), Northampton ('61-62), Crystal Palace ('62-65), Charlton ('65-66), Watford ('66), Orient ('66-67).
FA Cup runners'-up medal with Arsenal ('52). First player ever to be sold on HP when he moved from Arsenal to Watford. Most goals in a season for both Watford ('60) and Northampton ('62): 38 for Watford, 36 for

Northampton. Only post-war Northampton player to score a hat-trick on his debut.

HORNE, Alfred   Winger/wing half
Brixworth 6.9.1926
1   —   (4.1946-5.1949)
Northampton ('46-49), Corby, Wellingborough.

Ralph Hoten.

HOTEN, Ralph Vincent   Inside forward
Pinxton, Notts   Wellingborough
27.12.1896   1.2.1978
142   32   (12.1924-4.1928)
Notts County ('18-20), Portsmouth ('20-21), Luton ('21-24), Northampton ('24-28), Queens Park Rangers ('28-29).

HOULT, Alfred Aubrey   Wing half
Ashby-de-la-Zouch 9.7.1915
10   —   (9.1937-6.1938)
Notts County ('34-37), Northampton ('37-38).

George Hudson.

HUDSON, George Centre forward
Manchester 14.3.1937.
21   6   (3.1966-1.1967)
Blackburn ('58-60), Accrington ('60-61),
Peterborough ('61-64), Coventry ('64-66),
Northampton ('66-67), Tranmere ('67-69),
Altrincham.

HUFFER, Phillip Centre half
Bedworth 23.1.1932
1   —   (5.1954-5.1955)
Bedworth, Derby ('53-54), Northampton ('54-55).

Gwyn Hughes. (C&E)

HUGHES, Gwyn T. Wing half
Blaenau Festiniog 7.5.1922
281   26   (8.1944-5.1956)
Northampton ('44-56), Bedford, St Neots.
Recommended to Northampton by ex-'keeper, Len Hammond, made 42 appearances and eight goals during war. Played in all half back and forward positions for club. Represented Third Div south v north in the first-ever match between two leagues. Given a benefit in 1952.

HUNT, Robert R. Inside forward
Colchester 1.10.1942
47   15   (3.1963-9.1966)
                         (10.1972-1.1973 loan)
Colchester ('59-64), Northampton ('64-66), Millwall ('66-67), Ipswich ('67-70), Charlton ('70-73), Northampton ('72-73 loan), Reading ('73-75), Bury Town.
Most goals in a season for Colchester, 37 in

1962. Record fee for Colchester when he joined Northampton £25,000. Managed Colchester reserves and Bury Town.

Eli Hurel. (G)

HUREL, Eli Forward
Jersey 10.4.1915
14   2   (3.1938-9.1939)
Everton ('36-38), Northampton ('38-39).

HURRELL, William Defender
Newcastle 15.9.1955
5   —   Non contract
Northampton ('72-73).
Joined police force.

HUTCHINSON, Mark Midfield
Stoke 12.11.1963
2 + 1   —   (non contract)
Aston Villa ('80-83), Leicester ('83-85), Northampton ('85-86).

INGLIS, William Full back
Kirkaldy, 2.3.1897
64   —   (6.1930-6.1932)
Raith Rovers, Sheffield Wednesday ('24-25), Manchester United ('25-28), Northampton ('30-32).

INGRAM, Godfrey Forward
Luton 26.10.1959
10   4   (3.1980-5.1980 loan)
Luton ('77-81), Northampton ('80 loan), Cardiff ('81-82).
Ex-England Youth international, later joined the North American indoor league.

ISAAC, William H.   Goalkeeper
Pontypridd 16.5.1935
8   —   (7.1959-6.1960)
Stoke City ('53-56), Barry Town, Northampton ('59-60), Hereford ('60-).
Held several positions with Hereford since joining them in 1960, including player, manager, and physio and still employed by them today.

JACKSON, Leonard   Forward
Birmingham 6.9.1922
2   —   (7.1948-7.1949)
Birmingham ('46-48), Northampton ('48-49).

JAMES, Ronald   Forward
Birmingham 6.3.1922
4   1   (7.1948-7.1949)
Birmingham ('47-48), Northampton ('48-49).
Joined Northampton as part of the deal that took Archie Garrett to Birmingham.

Carl Jayes. (C&E)

JAYES, Carl   Goalkeeper
Leicester 15.3.1954
77   —   (11.1977-5.1980)
Leicester ('72-77), Northampton ('77-80), Leamington.
Quit the game to become a policeman.

JEFFREY, William   Midfield
Clydebank 25.10.1956
61 + 1   7   (3.1983-6.1984)
Oxford ('74-81), Blackpool ('81-83) Northampton ('83-84), Kettering, Rushden.

Tommy Jeffs.

JEFFS, Tommy Edmond   Full back
Peterborough 3.8.1900   Coventry 3.3.1971
160   —   (9.1971-5.1928)
Rugby Town, Northampton ('21-28).
Joined in 1921 as an amateur, but turned pro after one season.

JENKINS, Randolph   Forward
Sligo 5.9.1923
23   7   (6.1946-5.1948)
Walsall (war-'46), Northampton ('46-48), Fulham ('48-50), Gillingham ('50-51), Fulham ('51-52).

Harry Jennings. (G)

JENNINGS, Harold   Forward
Norwich 7.1.1920
15   2   (7.1939-5.1947)
Northampton ('39-47), Ipswich ('47-51),

Rochdale ('51), Crystal Palace ('51-52). Played three games, and scored one goal during war.

Jack Jennings. (C&E)

JENNINGS, Jack
War-time player, coach/trainer 1945-65.

JENNINGS, William   Wing half
Bulwell, Notts 25.2.1891
3   —   (10.1926-5.1927)
Luton ('20-26), Northampton ('26-27).

George Jobey.

JOBEY, George   Centre half
Heddon, Newcastle -.7.1885   Derby 9.3.1962
82   3   (7.1920-5.1922)
Newcastle ('05-12), Arsenal ('12-14), Bradford

('14-15), Hamilton, Leicester ('18-20), Northampton ('20-22).
FA Cup runners'-up medal with Newcastle 1912. Scored first ever goal at Highbury. Later managed Wolves, Derby, Mansfield.

JOHN, Malcolm   Forward
Bridgend 9.12.1950
36 + 7   9   (3.1973-5.1973 loan)
                         (10.1974-5.1975)
Swansea (amateur), Bristol Rovers ('71-74), Northampton ('74-75).

JOHNSON, Percy Raymond   Defender
Northampton   Northampton
13.12.1899   27.1.1983
12   —   (Amateur)
Northampton   ('21-23),   Higham,

JOHNSTON, Willie J.   Midfield
Sunderland 3.9.1948
— + 1   —   (8.1967-5.1968)
Sunderland (apprentice), Northampton ('67-68).
Member of the Sunderland Youth Cup winning side.

JONES, —   Forward
Local
1   1   (6.1935-5.1936)
Northampton ('35-36), Wellingborough.

JONES, Bernard   Forward
Coventry 10.4.1934
47   16   (10.1952-5.1956)
Northampton ('52-56), Cardiff City ('56-57), Shrewsbury Town ('57-59), Rugby Town.
One of the few Northampton players to score four goals in a game. Moved to Cardiff in exchange deal with Roland Williams and Colin Gale.

JONES, Bryn   Full back
Swansea 20.5.1931
7   —   (10.1963-11.1963)
Swansea   ('51-58),   Newport   ('58-60), Bournemouth ('60-63), Northampton ('63), Watford ('63-65).
Brother to Welsh international Cliff Jones. One of the shortest stays at Northampton: one month.

JONES, H.   Winger
Wolverton
5   8   (7.1926-5.1927)
Wolverton,   Northampton   ('26-27), Wolverton.

JONES, Robert   Midfield
Bristol 28.10.1938
19   1   (9.1966-2.1967)
Soundwell, Bristol Rovers ('56-66), Northampton ('66-67), Swindon ('67), Bristol Rovers ('67-71), Paulton Rovers.
Played for both Bristol Boys, and British Army. Moved to Swindon in exchange for Dennis Brown; later managed Bristol Rovers' youth side, and Bath City.

John Jones. (G)

JONES, John T.   Goalkeeper
Holywell 25.11.1916
81   —   (8.1938-8.1948)
Port Vale ('35-38), Northampton ('38-48), Oldham ('48-49).
Welsh schoolboy international. Played both sides of the war for Northampton. One of the Town's smallest 'keepers at 5 feet 9 inches.

JORDON, Gerry   Full back
Seaham 4.4.1949
1   —   (6.1966-6.1968)
Northampton ('66-68).

KANE, Peter   Forward
Petershill, Scotland 4.4.1939
49   25   (10.1959-7.1961)
                        (9.1963-4.1964)
Queens Park, Northampton ('59-60), Arsenal ('60-63), Northampton ('63-64), Crewe ('64-65), St Mirren.
Two spells at Northampton; later managed Barrow.

KENDALL, Mark   Goalkeeper
Nuneaton 10.12.1961
15   —   (7.1982-5.1983)
Aston Villa ('79-82), Northampton ('82-83), Birmingham ('83), Cardiff ('84-85).

KEY, Richard   Goalkeeper
Market Harborough 13.4.1956
2   —   (11.1982 loan)
Coventry (amateur), Exeter ('75-78), Cambridge United ('78-83), Northampton ('83 loan), Orient ('84 loan), Brentford ('85), Sunderland ('85 loan), Swindon ('86).
Returned to Cambridge to work on commercial side.

Joe Kiernan. (C&E)

KIERNAN, Joseph   Midfield
Coatbridge, Scotland 22.10.1942
348 + 2   15   (7.1963-5.1972)
Sunderland ('60-61), Northampton ('63-72), Kettering, Atherstone, Wellingborough.
Played in all four divisions for Northampton. Captained Kettering to the Southern League championship. Later coach to Irthlingborough Diamonds, and now coach to the Cobblers' youth team.

KILKELLY, Tom   Full back
Ireland 22.8.1955
2 + 2   —   (10.1974-11.1974 loan)
Leicester ('73-75), Northampton ('74 loan), Torquay ('75-76), Enderby Town.

KILSBY, Reginald H.   Forward
Wollaston 23.8.1910
1   —
Wellingborough, Northampton ('34-35), Scunthorpe, ('35-36), Rotherham ('36-37), Aldershot ('37-38), Tunbridge Wells, Rochdale ('39-40).

Bobby King. (G)

KING, F. A. Robert   Winger
Northampton 19.9.1919
101   23   (8.1937-5.1940)
                         (12.1947-5.1950)
Northampton ('37-39), Wolves ('39-47),
Northampton ('47-50), Rushden.
First wartime transfer, when he moved to
Wolves; returned as a replacement for Archie
Garrett in 1947; 22 wartime games and five
goals.

KIRKUP, Brian   Centre forward
Slough 16.4.1932
28   9   (7.1958-10.1959)
Bedford, Reading ('55-58), Northampton
('58-59), Aldershot ('59-60), Dover.

Brian Knight. (PN)

KNIGHT, Brian   Defender/midfield
Dundee 28.3.1949
10 + 3   —   (10.1969-5.1970)

Dundee, Huddersfield (trial), Northampton
('69-70), Cambridge City, Wellingborough
(player/manager), Bedford, Irthlingborough
Diamonds, Wellingborough (manager).
Now coach to Cobblers' reserves.

Tommy Knox.

KNOX, Tommy   Winger
Glasgow 5.4.1939
30 + 2   1   (12.1967-6.1969)
East Stirlingshire, Chelsea ('62-65), Newcastle
('65-67), Mansfield ('67), Northampton ('67-
69), St Mirren.

KRUSE, Patrick   Defender
Biggleswade 30.11.1953
18   —   (2.1982-5.1982 loan)
Leicester City ('72-74), Mansfield ('74-75),
Torquay ('75-77), Brentford ('77-82),
Northampton ('82 loan), Barnet.

KRYZWICKI, Richard   Winger/midfield
Flint 2.2.1947
8   3   (12.1973-1.1974)
West   Bromwich   Albion   ('67-70),
Huddersfield ('70-74), Scunthorpe ('74 loan),
Northampton ('74 loan), Lincoln ('74-75).
Welsh International.

John Kurila.

KURILA, John   Wing half
Glasgow 10.4.1941
158   4   (8.1962-5.1963)
                       (11.1963-6.1968)
Celtic, Northampton ('62-63), Hamilton
Steelers (Canada), Bristol City ('63),
Northampton ('63-68), Southend ('68-72),
Colchester ('72-74), Lincoln ('74-76),
Atherstone.
Two spells at Northampton. Signed for
Hamilton Steelers summer of 63, and could
not re-sign for Cobblers'; joined Bristol City
for three months, then rejoined
Northampton.

LAIRD, David   Inside forward
Cambusling 11.2.1936
14   1   (6.1960-6.1961)
St Mirren, Aldershot ('58-59), St Mirren,
Northampton ('60-61), Folkestone, Corby.
Teacher by profession. Scottish League Cup
runners'-up (St Mirren).

Frank Large.

LARGE, Frank   Centre forward
Leeds 26.1.1940
248   95   (3.1963-3.1964)
                        (12.1966-11.1967)
                        (8.1969-11.1972)
Halifax ('59-62), Queens Park Rangers ('62-
63), Northampton ('63-64), Swindon ('64),
Carlisle ('64-65), Oldham ('65-66),
Northampton ('66-67), Leicester ('67-68),
Fulham ('68-69), Northampton ('69-72),
Chesterfield ('72-73), Kettering.
Only player, during League days, to have
three spells at Northampton. Transfer values
for all moves over £150,000. From Leicester
to Fulham was makeweight in the Alan Clarke
deal, valued at £50,000; played some games
for Northampton at centre half. Second most
prolific scorer for post-war Northampton,
after Jack English. Now owns a farm in
County Mayo, Ireland.

John Lauderdale. (G)

50

**LAUDERDALE,
John Herbert**   Inside forward
Dumfries 27.11.1906
49   9   (11.1936-1.1939)
Queen of the South, Blackpool ('28-31),
Coventry ('31-36), Northampton ('36-39).
Third division South championship with
Coventry, 1936.

Derek Leck. (C&E)

LECK, Derek   Inside forward/Wing half
Northbourne 8.2.1937
267   49   (5.1958-11.1966)
Millwall ('55-58), Northampton ('58-65),
Brighton ('65-69), Hastings.
Converted to half back by Dave Bowen.
Scouted for Cobblers during '70s from the
south coast.

LEE, Trevor   Forward/midfield
London 3.7.1954
32   2   (7.1984-3.1985)
Epsom and Ewell, Millwall ('75-78),
Colchester ('78-81), Gillingham ('81-82),
Orient ('82), Bournemouth ('82-83), Cardiff
('83-84), Northampton ('84-85), Fulham ('85),
Epsom and Ewell.
A record fee was received when he moved
from Colchester to Gillingham for £90,000.

Ken Leek. (C&E)

LEEK, Kenneth   Inside forward
Ynysybwl 26.7.1935
94   32   (8.1952-5.1958)
                               (12.1964-11.1965)
Northampton ('52-58), Leicester ('58-61),
Newcastle ('61), Birmingham ('61-64),
Northampton ('64-65), Bradford City ('65-
67), Rhyl.
Welsh International: 13 caps; one under-23
cap. Granted benefit in 1958 with Roly Mills.
Hit headlines in 1961 as a Leicester player,
when he was left out of the Cup Final team v
Tottenham.

Gary Leonard. (C&E)

LEONARD, Gary Edward   Midfield
Northampton 23.3.1962
2   —   (apprentice)
Northampton ('79-81), Kettering, Long
Buckby, Cogenhoe.

Russell Lewis. (PN)

51

LEWIS, Russell   Centre half
Neath 15.9.1956
154 + 1   6   (6.1983-7.1986)
Everwarm, Swindon ('77-83), Northampton
('83-86), Kettering.
Northampton player-of-the-year, 1986.

LIDDLE, David   Midfield/defender
Malta 21.5.1957
35 + 3   3   (5.1975-5.1978)
Northampton ('77-79), Bedford, Milton
Keynes, Wellingborough, Buckingham.

LINCOLN, Andrew   Inside forward
Seaham Harbour   Seaham Harbour
17.5.1902   -.1.1977
2   —   (cs1928-5.1929)
Halifax ('22-24), Peterborough, Millwall ('27-
28), Northampton ('28-29), Stockport ('29-
31).

LINDSAY, Duncan Morton   Inside forward
Cambuslang -.-.1907
1   —   (9.1933-5.1934)
Cambuslang   Rangers,   East   Fife,
Cowdenbeath, Newcastle ('30-31), Bury ('31-
32), Ashington, Northampton ('33-34),
Hartlepool ('34-35), Barrow ('35-36), York
('36-37).
Once scored six goals in a game for
Cowdenbeath v St Johnstone.

LINES, Barry   Outside left
Bletchley 16.5.1942
284 + 8   50   (9.1960-5.1970)
Bletchley   Town,   Bletchley   United,
Northampton ('60-70), Milton Keynes.
First player to play and score in all four
divisions of the Football League, for the same
club; only player to be connected with the
Club's rise and fall from the Fourth Division
to their return.

LINNELL, John   Wing half
Holcot 2.1.1944
1   —   (9.1963-7.1967)
Northampton ('63-67), Peterborough ('67-
69).
County youth player 1962.

LITT, Steven   Midfield/defender
Carlisle 21.5.1954
21 + 1   —   (9.1977-3.1978)
Blackpool ('72), Luton ('72-74), Arsenal ('74
loan), Minnesota Kicks, Northampton ('77-
78), Minnesota Kicks.

LITTLE, John (Jack)   Full back
Gateshead 18.9.1904
59   1   (1.1936-5.1938)
Crook Town, Newcastle ('27-28), Southport
('28-33), Chester ('33-35), Le Harvre (France),
Northampton   ('35-38),   Exeter   ('38),
Fleetwood Hesketh.

Charlie Livesey. (C&E)

LIVESEY, Charles   Centre forward
West Ham 6.2.1938
33   5   (8.1964-10.1965)
Southampton   ('56-59),   Chelsea   ('59-61),
Gillingham   ('61-62),   Watford   ('62-64),
Northampton   ('64-65),   Brighton   ('65-69),
Crawley Town.

LLEWELLYN, Herbert   Centre forward
Godbourne 5.2.1939
2   —   (2.1963-2.1964)
Everton ('56-58), Crewe ('58-60), Port Vale
('60-63), Northampton ('63-64), Walsall ('64-
65).
England Youth International 1962. Debut for
Cobblers lasted only a few minutes, when he
was carried off v QPR.

LOASBY, Alan   Winger
Wellingborough 19.3.1937
2   —   (7.1958-6.1959)
Luton   ('54-58),   Northampton   ('58-59),
Wellingborough.
County youth player with Wellingborough
1953, Luton 1954.

Harry Loasby.

LOASBY, Harry　　　　　　　Forward
Wellingborough
31　　　　　　27　　　　　(5.1927-5.1930)
Wellingborough, Northampton ('27-30), Gillingham ('30-31), Luton ('31-32), Kettering.
Suffered a broken leg on two occasions. Best goal per game average ever for Northampton.

LOCKETT, William C.　　　Centre forward
Tipton, Staffs,　　　　　Market Harborough
23.4.1893　　　　　　　　　　25.9.1974
102　　　　　　78　　　　　(6.1914-5.1926)
Wolves ('13-14), Northampton ('14-26), Kidderminster.
England schoolboy International. Granted a benefit for Northampton v Southampton 1923. 76 Southern League games, with 32 goals.

Dave Logan. (PN)

LOGAN, David

David Longhurst. (PN)

LONGHURST, David

LOVATT, Harold　　　　　Inside forward
Audley, Staffs 1906
20　　　　　　11　　　　　(11.1931-5.1932)
Audley, Port Vale ('22-23), Preston North End ('23-24), Crewe ('24-25), Bradford City ('25-26), Wrexham ('26-27), Scarborough, Leicester ('28-29), Notts County ('29-31), Northampton ('31-32), Macclesfield, Stafford.

LOWERY, Harry　　　　　　Wing half
Moor Row, Cumberland 26.2.1918
92　　　　　　2　　　　　(10.1945-5.1949)
Cleaton Moor, West Bromwich Albion, ('36-45), Northampton ('45-49), Bromsgrove.
17 war games with one goal. Joined Cobblers in a three man, £4,500 deal in 1945.

LYMAN, Colin Charles　　　　Winger
Northampton　　　　　　　　Cambridge
9.3.1914　　　　　　　　　　-.5.1986
92　　　　　　30　　　　　(7.1934-10.1937)
West Bromwich Albion ('31-32), Rushden ('32-33), Southend ('33-34), Northampton ('34-38), Tottenham ('38-war), Port Vale ('46), Notts Forest ('46), Notts County ('46).
13 war time appearances with four goals. Joined Spurs for a 'near record' fee.

LYON, David   Defender
Northwick 18.1.1951
6   —   (10.1977-6.1978)
Bury ('69-71), Huddersfield ('71-73),
Mansfield ('73-74), Cambridge United ('74-
77), Northampton ('77-78), Cambridge City,
Wellingborough,   Buckingham,
Wellingborough.

MABEE, Gary L.   Forward
Oxford 1.2.1955
33 + 5   5   (8.1974-11.1975)
Tottenham ('72-74), Northampton ('74-75)
Retired through injury.

MACKIE, John Alexandra   Full back
Belfast 23.2.1903   Brentford 9.6.1984
11   —   (3.1936-7.1936)
Forth River (Ireland), Arsenal ('22-28),
Portsmouth ('28-36), Northampton ('36-37),
Hartlepool ('37-38), Chesterfield ('38-39).
Irish International, one cap. Div 3 south
championship medal with Portsmouth, 1924.
FA Cup runners'-up medals '29, '34, with
Portsmouth.

John Mackin. (C&E)

MACKIN, John   Utility
Glasgow 18.11.1943
103 + 7   13   (11.1963-6.1969)
Northampton ('63-69), Lincoln ('69), York
City ('69-73), Darlington ('73-76), Corby.
County youth cap '60-62, as a goalkeeper,
never missed a penalty for Northampton (6);
later managed Corby Town.

MAHONEY, Anthony   Forward
Tilbury 29.9.1959
11   3   (10.1981-12.1981 loan)
Fulham ('79-82), Northampton ('81 loan),

Brentford ('82-84), Crystal Palace ('84-85),
Barnet.
Did not score in six League games, but scored
three times in five Cup games. Loan period
was cancelled when he failed to show for an
away game v Peterborough.

MALCOLM, Alexander   Full back
Hamilton 13.2.1956
2   —   (7.1976-7.1977)
Luton ('74-76), Northampton ('76-77),
Dunstable, Hitchin.

Bob Maloney.

MALONEY, Robert   Centre half
Thurlaston, Leicester   -.1.1981
194   4   (11.1926-3.1932)
Thurlaston, Walsall ('25-26), Peterborough,
Northampton ('26-32), Dundalk, Racing Club
Paris.
Cost Northampton £1,000 together with
Allon. Granted a benefit v Grimsby, 1932.

Adrian Mann. (PN)

MANN, Adrian   Midfield
Northampton 12.7.1967
83 + 15   6   (7.1984-11.1987)
Northampton ('83-87), Southampton ('85 loan), Torquay ('86 loan), Bath ('87 loan), Altrincham ('87 loan), Newport ('87-88), Wycombe Wanderers, Aylesbury.
County youth player 1984. Youngest player to play for Northampton: 16 years 297 days.

MARSTON, Maurice   Full back
Trindon, Durham 24.3.1929
155   2   (7.1953-5.1957)
Sunderland ('49-53), Northampton ('53-57), Kettering.
Later became Kettering Town Secretary, until a few years ago.

Don Martin. (C&E)

MARTIN, Donnah   Utility
Corby 15.2.1944
238 + 15   80   (3.1962-2.1968)
                       (9.1975-5.1978)
Northampton ('62-67), Blackburn ('67-75), Northampton ('75-78), Dunstable, Corby (player manager).
County youth cap 1962, England Youth International. A fractured jaw robbed him of a possible England under-21 cap. Two spells at Northampton; wore every outfield shirt except 3.

MARTINEZ, Eugene   Midfield
Chelmsford 6.7.1957
12   2   (2.1984-4.1984 loan)
Bradford City ('77-80), Rochdale ('80-82), Newport ('82-84), Northampton ('84 loan).

Steve Massey.

MASSEY, Steven   Forward
Denton, Manchester 28.3.1958
82   30   (2.1982-6.1983)
Stockport ('76-79), Bournemouth ('79-80), Peterborough ('80-81), Northampton ('81-83), Hull City ('83-85), Cambridge United ('85-86), Wrexham ('86-).
FA Tribunal set his fee to Hull at £20,000.

MATTHEWS, Paul W.   Midfield
Leicester City 30.9.1946
13   —
Leicester ('64-72), Southend ('72 loan), Mansfield ('72-77), Rotherham ('77-79), Northampton ('79 loan).

MAXWELL, Kenneth   Wing half
Partick 11.2.1928
2   (6.1949-5.1951)
Kilmarnock, Northampton ('49-57), Bradford ('57-58), Albion Rovers.

MAYES, Alan K.   Forward
Edmonton 11.12.1953
10   4   (1.1976-3.1976 loan)
Queens Park Rangers ('71-74), Watford ('74-76), Northampton ('76 loan), Swindon ('76-79), Chelsea ('79-80), Swindon ('80-84), Carlisle ('84-85), Blackpool ('85-87), Wycombe Wanderers.

MEAD, Peter   Full back
Luton 9.9.1956
81 + 3   4   (7.1977-6.1979)
Luton ('76-77), Northampton ('77-79), Hitchin, Aylesbury.
Only Northampton player to make his debut on his 21st birthday.

MELANIPHY, Eugene M. I.   Forward
Westport, Mayo 5.2.1912
3   1   (7.1939-9.1939)
Finchley ('31-35), Plymouth ('35-37), Cardiff ('37-39), Northampton ('39).
Guest for Tranmere during the war.

MELVILLE, James   Centre half
Barrow 15.3.1909   Coventry 2.8.1961
22   1   (3.1934-5.1936)
Barrow (amateur), Blackburn ('28-33), Hull ('33-34), Northampton ('34-36).
Slow left-arm bowler with Warwickshire in 1946.

MILLAR, John   Full back
Coatbridge 8.12.1966
4   —   (1.1987 loan)
Chelsea ('84-87), Hamilton ('86 loan), Northampton ('87 loan), Blackburn ('87-).
Only four games for Northampton, but appeared in three competitions: League, FA Cup and Freight Rover Trophy.

MILLER, Harold Sidney (Dusty)   Wing half
Watford 20.5.1902
3   —   (6.1939-9.1939)
St Albans, Charlton ('21-23), Chelsea ('23-29), Northampton ('39).
England Amateur International.

MILLER, Roger L.   Winger
Moulton 18.8.1938
4   1   (11.1956-5.1959)
Northampton ('56-59), Wellingborough.

Roly Mills. (C&E)

MILLS, Roland W. G.   Utility
Daventry 22.6.1933
324   33   (5.1951-5.1964 as a player)
Northampton ('51-65)
County youth cap 1950; England Youth International. Represented Div 3 south v north. Became assistant trainer in 1965; still connected with the Club on the promotions side.

MITCHELL, Albert J.   Winger
Stoke 22.1.1922
90   29   (5.1949-5.1951)
Burslem Albion, Stoke ('47-48), Blackburn ('48-49), Kettering, Northampton ('49-51), Luton ('51-55), Middlesbrough ('55-56), Southport ('56-57), Wellington, Kiddermister.
England 'B' International. When he joined Northampton, a split fee had to be paid to both Kettering and Blackburn.

MITCHELL, Andrew   Winger
Coxhoe, Durham   Blackburn
20.4.1907   3.12.1971
18   3   (12.1933-5.1934)
Crook Town, Sunderland ('27-28), Notts County ('28-29), Darlington ('29-32), Manchester United ('32-33), Hull City ('33), Northampton ('33-34).

MOLLOY, W.   Winger
3   —
Spon, Northampton ('24-25)

Graham Moore. (C&E)

MOORE, Graham   Midfield
Glamorgan 7.3.1941
58 + 1   12   (12.1965-6.1967)
Cardiff ('58-61), Chelsea ('61-63), Manchester United ('63-65), Northampton ('65-67), Charlton ('67-71), Doncaster ('71-74).
Welsh International: 21 caps; nine under-23 caps; also represented the Football League.

MOORE, John   Defender
Harthill, Scotland 21.12.1943
16   —   (8.1974-8.1975)
Motherwell, Luton ('65-72), Brighton ('72 loan), Northampton ('74-75), Hitchin.
Managed Luton for a season, after David Pleat left, but resigned.

MORAN, James   Inside forward
Wishaw 6.3.1935
25   7   (1.1961-8.1962)
Wishaw, Leicester ('55-57), Norwich ('57-61), Northampton ('61-62), Darlington ('62-63), Workington ('63-64).

Trevor Morley. (PN)

MORLEY, Trevor   Forward
Nottingham 20.3.1962
130   45   (5.1985-1.1988)
Derby County ('80-81), Corby, Nuneaton, Northampton ('85-88), Manchester City ('88). England semi-professional International. Division Four Championship medal. Cost £30,000 on a joint fee; moved for over £200,000.

MORRALL, Alfred Douglas   Forward
Dudderston 1.7.1916
45   19   (12.1945-6.1948)
Redditch, Northampton ('44-48), Newport ('48-50).
Son of Alf Morrall, late of Hull City, made 57 League war-time appearances with 25 goals.

MORRITT, Gordon A.   Goalkeeper
Rotherham 8.2.1942
46   —   (8.1968-11.1969)
Rotherham ('61-65), South Africa, Doncaster ('67-68), Northampton ('68-69), York City ('69-72), Rochdale ('72-73), Darlington ('73-74).
One of the tallest 'keepers on the Cobblers' books at 6 feet 4 inches.

MORROW, Hugh   Winger
Larne, Northern Ireland 9.7.1930
30   3   (7.1956-5.1957)
West Bromwich Albion ('48-50), Lockheed Hudson, Nuneaton, Lockheed Leamington, Northampton ('56-57), Kettering, Tamworth (player/manager).
Managed several of the Midland Junior teams.

MORTIMER, Robert   Forward
Bolton, -.-.1909
66   24   (12.1931-6.1933)
Bolton ('27-29), Barrow ('29-30), Bolton ('30-31), Northampton ('31-33), Brentford ('33-34), Bournemouth ('34-35), Accrington ('35-38), Portsmouth ('38), Blackburn ('38), York ('38), Accrington ('39).

MUIR, M.   Full back
Campbelltown
3   —   (7.1930-6.1931)
Aberdeen, Northampton ('30-31).

MUIR, Maurice   Midfield
Wimbledon 19.3.1963
18 + 18   1   (Non contract)
Crystal Palace (schoolboy), Northampton ('79-80), Leamington, Banbury, Northampton

('81-84), Kettering, Wellingborough.
England schoolboy International. Two spells at Northampton, both as a non-contract player; recommended to Northampton by Ted Drake.

Tommy Mulgrew. (C&E)

MULGREW, Tommy   Inside forward
Motherwell 13.4.1929
8   1   (7.1949-10.1952)
Morton, Northampton ('49-52), Newcastle ('52-54), Southampton ('54-62), Aldershot ('62-65), Andover.
Moved to Newcastle for £8,000. Was a 'saint' and a 'sinner' at Southampton; he scored within 15 seconds of his debut, but was also the first Southampton player to be sent off for 29 years.

Brian Mundee. (PN)

MUNDEE, Brian   Full back
London 12.1.1964
114 + 4   4   (8.1983-3.1986)
Hungerford Town, Bournemouth ('81-83), Northampton ('83-86), Cambridge United ('86-87), Maidstone, Weymouth, Poole.
England Youth International. When at Weymouth, had to take over in goal on his debut, and saved a penalty.

MURPHY, Edward (Eddie)   Inside forward
Hamilton 13.5.1924
79   16   (6.1949-3.1951)
Hibernians, Morton, Northampton ('49-51), Barnsley ('51-52), Exeter ('52-54).
Scottish League Cup finalist with Morton. Moved to Barnsley for a 'near record' fee, paid for with the money they received from the Danny Blanchflower sale to Aston Villa.

Colin Myers.

MYERS, Colin E.   Inside forward
Wortley -.7.1984
80   32   (7.1922-10.1924)
Hickleton, Bradford City ('19-20), Southend ('20-21), Aberdare ('21-22), Northampton ('22-25), Queens Park Rangers ('24-25), Exeter ('25-26), Hartlepool ('26-27), Gainsborough Trinity, Grantham.

McCAFFREY, James   Midfield/winger
Luton 12.10.1951
61 + 1   7   (12.1978-5.1980)
Notts Forest ('69-72), Mansfield ('72-77), Huddersfield ('77-78), Portsmouth ('78),

Northampton ('78-80).
England Youth International. Retired to run a newsagents in the North.

McALEER, Joseph   Outside right
Scotland
8   6   (7.1933-5.1934)
Arbroath, Rochdale ('31-33), Glenavon, Northampton ('33-34), Lincoln ('34-35), Orient ('35-36), Gillingham ('36-37), Wrexham ('37-38).
Believed to be only Cobbler to have played in all four home countries.

Jason McCartney. (G)

McCARTNEY, Jason James   Winger
Washington, Durham   Newcastle
30.3.1909   16.2.1976
24   7   (9.1938-5.1939)
Washington Colliery, Newcastle ('28-29), Swindon ('29-31), Bath, Wardley, Millwall ('37-38), Northampton ('38-39).

McCOY, Wilf (Tim)   Centre half
Brighton 4.3.1921
69   —   (12.1948-1.1951)
Portsmouth ('46-48), Northampton ('48-51), Brighton ('51-56), Tonbridge.

Adam McCulloch. (C&E)

McCULLOCH, Adam Alexander
  Bell Ross   Centre forward
Crossford 4.6.1920
99   39   (6.1949-1.1952)
Third Lanark, Northampton ('49-51), Shrewsbury ('51-53), Aldershot ('53-56), Ramsgate.
Emigrated to Australia, but later returned. Son Andy, born in Northampton, played for several League clubs in the '70s.

McCULLOCH, Thomas   Outside right
Scotland 25.12.1921
2   —   (10.1949-5.1950)
Airdrie, Queen of the South, Northampton ('49-51), Bradford City ('51-54), Crewe ('54-55).

Keillor McCullough. (G)

McCULLOUGH, Keillor   Full back
Larne
41   2   (3.1938-9.1939)
Belfast Celtic, Manchester City ('35-38), Northampton ('38-40).
Irish International. Made 21 wartime appearances for Northampton.

McFARLANE, James   Forward
—
3   1
Liverpool ('28-30), Aberdeen, Northampton ('32-33), Kidderminster, Darlington ('35-37).

McGLEISH, John   Outside right
Lanark 9.11.1951
7 + 1   —   (12.1969-5.1973)
Northampton ('69-73).

McGOLDRICK, Eddie John Paul

McGOWAN, Andrew   Midfield
Corby 17.5.1956
99 + 12   15   (7.1975-5.1978)
Corby Town, Northampton ('75-78),
Irthlingborough Diamonds, Stamford,
Rushden, Corby, Kidderminster, Kettering.
County youth cap; England Youth
International, 1974. Retired from League
football due to a leg injury.

McGUIRE, James   Centre half
Edinburgh -.-.1911
86   —   (4.1932-6.1939)
Celtic ('28-30), Brooklyn Wanderers (USA),
Northampton ('32-39).
Scottish schoolboy International. Capped by
USA.
Although he did not play in his last three
seasons here, the Club held his registration.
Spent all his summers in USA, later emigrated
there and helped to set up soccer in the States.

McILVENNY, Patrick   Outside right
Belfast -.-.1900
8   2   (9.1928-6.1929)
Distillery, Cardiff ('24-25), Sheffield
Wednesday ('25-26), Shelbourne,
Northampton ('28-29).

McKECHNIE, John P.   Full back
Inverness
11   —   (6.1920-5.1921)
Newcastle ('19-20), Northampton ('20-21),
Exeter ('21-23), Orient ('23-26).

McKEE, Ray   Goalkeeper
Finchley 16.2.1926
5   —   (Amateur)
Finchley Town, Northampton ('46-47).

McKENNA, Mike   Wing half
Birmingham
4   —   (7.1946-5.1947)
Bromsgrove, Northampton ('46-47).

McLACHLIN, Edward Roland   Winger
Glasgow 24.9.1903   Leicester 16.3.1970
11   1   (7.1930-5.1931)
Third Lanark, Leicester ('25-26), Mansfield
('26-30), Northampton ('30-31), Mansfield
('31-32).

McLAIN, Thomas   Wing half
Linton 19.1.1922
97   11   (6.1952-5.1956)

Ashington, Sunderland ('46-52),
Northampton ('52-56), Headington,
Wellingborough (player/manager).
A qualified FA coach, represented the
Football Combination v a Dutch XI. Joined
Northampton for £3,000; later returned
north, and became a sales representative.

McMENEMY, Frank   Wing half
Lanarkshire -.-.1910
66   3   (2.1934-5.1936)
Hamilton, Tunbridge Wells, Airdrie,
Northampton ('33-36), Crystal Palace ('36-37).

McMENEMY, Paul   Forward
Farnboro' 5.11.1966
4   2   (1.1987-2.1987 loan)
West Ham United ('84-87), Aldershot ('86
loan), Northampton ('87 loan), Bromley.

Bill McNaughton.

**McNAUGHTON,
William Fredrick**   Forward
Barking 8.12.1905   27.8.1980
12   2   (5.1928-5.1930)
Barking, Millwall ('25-26), Peterborough,
Northampton ('28-30), Gateshead ('30-32),
Hull ('32-34), Stockport ('34-36).
Represented Essex County. Div 3 North top
scorer for Hull, 1933 with 41 goals; Third
Division North championship with Hull 1933.

Dixie McNeil.

McNEIL, Richard (Dixie)   Forward
Melton Mowbray 16.1.1947
104 + 1   38   (7.1969-1.1972)
Holwell Works, Leicester ('64-66), Exeter ('66-67), Corby, Northampton ('69-72), Lincoln ('72-74), Hereford ('74-77), Wrexham ('77-81), Hereford ('81-82).
Holds Div 3 championship medals with both Hereford and Wrexham.
Became manager of Wrexham.

McPARTLAND, Desmond   Goalkeeper
Middlesbrough 5.10.1947
6   —   (7.1969-3.1970)
Middlesbrough ('64-67), Carlisle ('67-69), Northampton ('69-70), Hartlepool ('70-71).

Keith McPherson. (PN)

McPHERSON, Keith Anthony (Macca)

NEAL, George   Wing half
Wellingborough
3   —   (cs1944-5.1947)
Northampton ('44-47).
Also made 34 wartime appearances.

Phil Neal. (C&E)

NEAL, Phillip   Utility
Irchester 20.2.1951
201 + 6   31   (12.1968-10.1974)
Northampton ('68-75), Liverpool ('75-86), Bolton Wanderers (86-).
England International: 50 caps; ex-County youth cap. Won every domestic honour except the FA Cup; holds European Cup medal. Played in *every* shirt for Northampton, including stand-in 'keeper. Now manager of Bolton Wanderers.

NEBBELING, Gavin   Centre half
Johannesburg 15.5.1963
12   —   (10.1985-1.1986 loan)
Arcadia Shepherds, Crystal Palace ('82-), Northampton ('85-86 loan). Only South African to play for the Club.

NEEDHAM, George Wright   Wing half
Staveley
37   1   (2.1924-4.1925)
Staveley, Sheffield United (12-13), Staveley, Luton (14-15), Sherwood Foresters, Derby ('20-21), Gillingham ('21-23), Northampton ('23-25).
Nephew to the ex-Sheffield United and England player, Ernest 'Nudger' Needham.

NEWMAN, Ronald   Forward
Pontypridd 1.5.1933
18   5   (10.1953-3.1956)

Northampton ('53-56), Coventry ('56-57), Torquay ('57-58), Bedford, Rugby Town, Rushden Town.
Joined Coventry in an exchange deal with Charlie Dutton.

Frank Newton.

NEWTON, Frank   Wing half
Menston, Yorks -.10.1894
46   1   (2.1923-2.1924)
Burnley ('14-15), Clyde, Menston, Bradford City ('21-22), Northampton ('22-24), Halifax ('24-26).

NORRIS, Oliver   Wing half
Londonderry 1.4.1929
15   1   (9.1958-4.1959)
Middlesbrough ('48-55), Bournemouth ('55-58), Northampton ('58-59), Ashford Town, Rochdale ('60-61), Gloucester City (player/manager), Hakouk (Australia).
Known as the clown prince of soccer. Actually scored for the Cobblers before joining them when, in an FA Cup match for Bournemouth, he scored an own goal. Emigrated to Australia.

OAKLEY, James Ernest   Full back
Tynemouth   Northumberland
10.11.1901   -.7.1972
35   (3.1931-5.1933)
Blyth Spartans, Sunderland ('22-30), Reading ('30-31), Northampton ('31-33), Kettering.

OAKLEY, Kenneth   Centre forward
Cardiff 9.5.1929
13   6   (7.1954-5.1955)
Cardiff ('46-49), Ebbw Vale, Cardiff ('50-54), Northampton ('54-55), Ebbw Vale.

George O'Dell.

O'DELL, George W.   Wing half
Hoddesdon, Herts
161   10   (6.1927-3.1932)
St Albans, Northampton ('27-32), Wigan ('32-34), Newport ('34-35).

O'DONAGHUE, Michael   Forward
London 13.9.1956
4   1   (11.1979-12.1979 loan)
Wembley,   Southampton   ('74-79), Northampton ('79 loan).
Emigrated to Australia.

O'DONNELL, Christopher   Full back
Newcastle 26.5.1968
1   —   (1.1988 loan)
Ipswich ('86-), Northampton ('88 loan).

O'DONNELL, William   Centre forward
Clydebank 9.8.1924
109   43   (6.1951-6.1954)
Partick, Northampton ('51-54), Shrewsbury ('54-58).

OLHA, Bela   Inside forward
Hungary, 8.6.1938
44   8   (12.1958-12.1960)
Bedford, Northampton ('58-60), Wisbech, Hastings.

OMAN, Alan   Full back
Newcastle 6.10.1952
91 + 5   3   (10.1970-5.1975)
Northampton ('69-76), Wellingborough.

O'NEILL, Joseph   Wing half
Glasgow 15.8.1931
28   4   (10.1957-5.1959)
Aberdeen, Southend ('54-), Aberdeen,
Leicester ('56-57), Northampton ('57-59),
Bath.

O'NEILL, Thomas   Midfield
Glasgow 2.2.1958
51   7   (7.1983-5.1984)
Ipswich ('75-76), Cambridge ('76-83),
Northampton ('83-84), Royston.

John O'Rourke. (G)

O'ROURKE, James (John)   Full back
Bolton
10   —   (6.1936-5.1939)
Bury ('35-36), Northampton ('37-39).

O'ROURKE, Peter (Junior)   Inside forward
Newmains 14.3.1903
2   —   (7.1925-6.1926)
Bradford ('24-25), Northampton ('25-26),
Norwich ('26-27).
Later managed Bradford.

OWEN, Robert   Midfield
Farnworth 17.10.1947
5   —   (10.1976-11.1976 loan)
Bury ('65-68), Manchester City ('68-70),
Carlisle ('70-76), Swansea ('70 loan),
Northampton ('76 loan), Workington ('76
loan), Bury ('77 loan), Doncaster ('77-79).
Each of the clubs he played for in 1976 either
suffered relegation or re-election.

OXLEY, Richard Lambert   Defender
Wallsend -.1.1895   Wallsend 3.7.1953
1   —   (10.1924-5.1925)
Wallsend, Accrington ('21-22), Southport
('22-23), Queens Park Rangers ('23-24),
Northampton ('24-25).

OXLEY, William   Forward
Wallsend
1   —   (5.1926-5.1927)
Rochdale ('22-23), Manchester United ('23-
24), Southport ('24-25), Merthyr ('25-26),
Northampton ('26-27), Durham, Wigan.

Lois Page.

PAGE, Lois A.   Winger
Kirkdale, Lancs   Birkenhead
-.4.1899   12.10.1959
130   27   (cs1922-6.1925)
South Liverpool, Stoke ('19-22),
Northampton ('22-25), Burnley ('25-32),
Manchester United ('32-), Port Vale ('32-33).
England International, seven caps, one goal.
Represented Football League v Irish League.
When he joined Burnley, Jack Tresadern
came the other way, as player/manager. He
also managed Yeovil ('33-35), Newport ('35-
37), Glentoran ('37-39), Swindon ('45-53),
Chester ('53-56).

PAGE, William   Inside forward
Lancs 19.9.1896   3.12.1981
13   1   12.1922-5.1923
Cardiff ('17-22), Northampton ('22-23).
Brother to Lois.

PARK, Oswald (Ollie) Centre half
Darlington 7.2.1905
75 — (6.1931-5.1935)
Darlington Railway, Newcastle ('24-31), Connas Quay ('29-30), Northampton ('31-34), Hartlepool ('34-38), Consett (player/ manager).

PARK, Robert Midfield
Edinburgh 3.7.1946
22 + 4 — (2.1973-7.1974)
Aston Villa ('63-69), Wrexham ('69-72), Peterborough ('72-73), Northampton ('73-74), Hartlepool ('74-76).

PARKER, Kenneth Defender
Newcastle -.-.1954
1 — (non-contract)
Northampton ('71-74), Milton Keynes, Bedford.

John Parris. (G)

PARRIS, John Edward (Eddie) Winger
Chepstow 31.1.1911
26 7 (11.1937-6.1939)
Bradford ('28-34), Bournemouth ('34-36), Luton ('36-37), Northampton ('37-39).
First coloured player to play League football for Northampton (Walter Tull played for the club in the Southern League). Welsh International (one cap), five wartime games and one goal.

PARTON, Jeffrey Goalkeeper
Swansea 24.2.1953
29 — (6.1975-6.1978)
Burnley ('71-75), Northampton ('75-78), Irthlingborough Diamonds, Welsh under-23 International.

PARTRIDGE, Albert Edward Winger
Birmingham 13.2.1901 Shipley 11.11.1966
2 — (9.1933-5.1934)
Newcastle ('27-29), Redditch, Sheffield United ('30-32), Bradford City ('32-33), Northampton ('33-34).

PATCHING, Martin Midfield
Rotherham 1.11.1958
6 1 (1.1983-2.1983 loan)
Wolves ('76-80), Watford ('80-83), Northampton ('82-83 loan).
Retired in 1983 through injury, and took a pub.

Ron Patterson. (C&E)

PATTERSON, Ronald L. Full back
Gateshead 30.10.1929
318 5 (6.1952-6.1962)
Crystal Palace (apprentice), Middlesbrough ('49-52), Northampton ('52-62), Rothwell Town (player/manager).
Fully qualified FA coach. Given a testimonial on his release, and later managed Hendon.

Joe Payne. (C&E)

Billy Pease.

PAYNE, Irving E. H. (Joe)   Inside forward
Britton Ebray, Swansea 29.6.1921
33   7   (8.1951-5.1952 as a player)
Swansea ('46-49), Newport ('49-50), Scunthorpe ('50-51), Northampton ('51-53). Coach to the Cobblers' Colts ('53-55); second team trainer ('56-66); first team coach ('66-68).

PEACOCK, Robert   Wing half
Rushden 18.12.1937
3   —   (2.1957-5.1958)
Rushden Town, Northampton ('56-58), Kettering, Rushden Town.

PEASE, William Harold   Winger
Leeds, 30.9.1899   Redcar 2.10.1955
268   51   (10.1919-6.1926)
Leeds ('18-19), Northampton ('19-26), Middlesbrough ('26-33), Luton ('33-35).
England International. Division Two championship with Middlesbrough 1927 & 1929. 32 Southern League games and two goals.

PERKINS, Glen S.   Midfield
Little Billing 12.10.1960
— + 1   —   (10.1978-5.1979)
Northampton ('78-79).

PERRIN, Steven   Forward
London 13.2.1952
22 + 1   6   (12.1982-12.1983)
Wycombe Wanderers, Crystal Palace ('76-78), Plymouth ('78-79), Portsmouth ('79-80), Hillingdon Borough, Northampton ('81-83), Wycombe Wanderers, Hillingdon Borough, St Albans.
A schoolteacher by profession.

PERRY, Michael   Forward
Wimbledon 4.4.1964
4   —   (12.1984-1.1985 loan)
West Bromwich Albion ('82-85), Northampton ('84-85 loan), Torquay ('85-86), Stafford Rangers, Wealdstone.

PERRYMAN, Raymond   Full back
West Haddon 3.10.1947
1   —   (9.1966-6.1968)
Northampton ('66-68), Colchester ('68-69).

PHILLIPS, Ian A.   Full back
Edinburgh 23.4.1959
55   1   (7.1982-9.1983)
Ipswich ('77-79), Mansfield ('79-80), Peterborough ('80-82), Northampton ('82-84), Colchester ('84-87), Aldershot ('87-).

PHILLIPS, Ralph   Full back
Durham 9.8.1933
89   1   (8.1958-6.1961)
Middlesbrough ('54-58), Northampton ('58-61), Darlington ('61-63).

PHILLIPS, Steven   Forward
Islington 4.8.1954
140 + 1   42   (10.1975-2.1977)
                      (8.1980-3.1982)
Birmingham ('72-75), Torquay ('74 loan), Northampton ('75-77), Brentford ('77-80), Northampton ('81-82), Southend ('82-85), Torquay ('85-86 loan), Peterborough ('86-), Exeter ('87 loan), Chesterfield ('88 loan).
Ex-England Youth International. First came to the County ground as a loan player, playing in midfield; cost £40,000 on his return in 1980, at the time a record fee.

PICKERING, Peter   Goalkeeper
York 24.3.1926
91   —   (7.1955-12.1957)
Earswick, York City ('46-48), Chelsea ('48-52), Kettering, Northampton ('55-58).
Saved seven penalties in 50 games for York. His move to Chelsea cost £20,000, the most money paid for a 'keeper at the time. Had one game for Northamptonshire CC v Leicestershire as a right-hand batsman. Emigrated to South Africa in 1957 and became a cricket umpire.

PINCHBECH, Clifford B.   Centre forward
Cleethorpes 20.1.1925
3   3   (12.1951-5.1953)
Scunthorpe, Everton ('47-49), Brighton ('49), Port Vale ('49-51), Northampton ('51-53), Bath City.
A broken ankle ended his League career, after just three first team outings.

Richard Platt. (G)

PLATT, Richard   Full back
Huyton
5   —   (8.1937-9.1939)
Huyton Quarry, Tranmere ('35-37), Northampton ('37-39).

Andy Poole. (C&E)

POOLE, Andrew   Goalkeeper
Chesterfield 6.7.1960
157   —   (7.1978-6.1982)
Mansfield ('77-78), Northampton ('78-82), Wolves ('82), Port Vale ('82), Gillingham ('83), Nuneaton, Coventry Sporting, Worcester City, Bedworth, Kettering.

POOLE, Kenneth   Wing half
Blancwm (Wales) 2.7.1933
4   —   (6.1956-5.1957)
Swansea ('53-56), Northampton ('56-57)

POOLE, Kevin   Goalkeeper
Bromsgrove 21.7.1965
3   —   (10.1984-12.1984 loan)
Aston Villa ('83-87), Northampton ('85 loan),
Middlesbrough ('87-).

POPPY, Arthur   Midfield
Yeovil 6.1.1961
1   —   (non-contract)
Northampton ('77-78).

Tom Postlethwaite. (G)

POSTLETHWAITE,
Thomas William   Wing half
Haverthwaite, Lancs 4.9.1909
65   1   (6.1937-7.1939)
Barrow ('31-34), Bradford ('34-37),
Northampton ('37-38).

POTTER, F. Len   Forward
Bedford
20   6   (10.1934-5.1936)
Bedford, Northampton ('34-36),
Wellingborough.

John Potts. (C&E)

POTTS, Henry James   Winger
Carlisle 23.1.1925
10   —   (Amateur)
Oxford University, Pegasus, Northampton
('50), Kettering.
England Amateur International. Played first-
class cricket for Oxford University, winning a
'blue'. Later became a Kettering Magistrate.

POYNTZ, William Ivor   Forward
Taylorstown, Glamorgan   Leeds
18.3.1894   5.4.1966
30   5   (cs1924-6.1925)
(
Llanelly, Leeds ('21-23), Doncaster ('23-24),
Northampton ('24-25), Bradford ('25-26),
Crewe ('26-27), Hartlepool ('27-28).
While a Leeds player, scored a hat-trick three
hours after he was married.

PRICE, Eric   Forward
Hemsworth 3.9.05   Congleton -.1.1976
4   2   (5.1927-5.1928)
Manchester City ('24-26), Norwich ('26-27),
Northampton ('27-28), Torquay United ('28-
29).

PRICE, Raymond   Centre forward
Northampton 30.11.1948
7   —   (12.1966-5.1968)
Northampton ('66-68), Corby.

QUINNEY, Henry James   Full back
Rugby 15.10.1922
3   —   (3.1944-7.1947)
Wolves (amateur), Northampton ('44-47),
Banbury.
Also made one wartime appearance.

RADFORD, Bernard   Utility
West Melton -.-.1907
7   —   (6.1931-7.1932)
Darefield, Nelson ('27-30), Sheffield United
('30-31), Northampton ('31-32).

Freddie Ramscar.

RAMSCAR, Fredrick T.   Inside forward
Salford 24.1.1919
146   59   (7.1951-9.1954)
Stockport ('44-46), Wolves ('46-47), Queens Park Rangers ('47-49), Preston North End ('49-51), Northampton ('51-54), Millwall ('54-55), Peterborough, Northampton (Colts coach), Wellingborough.
Guested for Stockport and Queens Park Rangers during the war. The day after he signed for Stockport was offered terms by Manchester United. Colts coach for many seasons; actually played in the side. Now living in retirement in Northampton.

Frank Rankmore. (C&E)

RANKMORE, Frank   Centre half
Cardiff 21.7.1939
123   19   (6.1968-5.1971)
Cardiff Corries, Cardiff ('57-63), Peterborough ('63-68), Northampton ('68-71).
Welsh International (one cap). Retired in 1971 with an injury that also cost the club promotion by his loss. Took a public house in Northampton, before returning to Cardiff.

RAWLINGS, Charles James Sidney   Winger
Wombwell 5.5.1913   Penarth 10.7.1956
53   19   (7.1936-12.1937)
Preston North End ('31-33), Huddersfield ('33-34), West Bromwich Albion ('34-36), Northampton ('36-37), Millwall ('37-39), Everton (war-'46), Plymouth ('46-48).
Father Archie, played for Northampton in the Southern League days. Played for Orient, Rochdale and Bury as a guest during the war.

Graham Reed. (P.N)

REED, Graham (Rambo)

REID, John   Inside forward
Newmains, 20.8.1932
90   16   (11.1961-11.1963)
Hamilton, Bradford City ('57-61), Northampton ('61-63), Luton ('63-66), Torquay ('66-67), Rochdale ('67-68).
Division Three championship medal with Northampton; returned to Bradford to take up a newsagents.

REILLY, George   Centre forward/half
Belshill 14.9.1957
141+3   55   (8.1976-11.1979)
Corby Town, Northampton ('76-79), Cambridge United ('79-83), Watford ('83-84), Newcastle ('84-86), West Bromwich Albion ('86-), Cambridge ('88).
County youth cap with Corby '76, '77, '78. FA Cup runners'-up medal with Watford 1984. Was Cobblers' most expensive player when they sold him to Cambridge, for £160,000.

Len Riches.

RICHES, Leonard Arthur   Wing half
Broughton, Kettering -.-.1910
148   9   (6.1929-6.1938)
Kettering, Northampton ('29-38), Kettering.

RIDDICK, Gordon   Midfield
Watford 6.11.1943
28   3   (12.1972-10.1973)
Luton ('61-67), Gillingham ('67-69), Charlton ('69-70), Orient ('70-72), Northampton ('72-73), Brentford ('73-76).
First player transferred after Bill Dodgin came, as he wanted to be near his building business in Herts.

RILEY, Harold   Winger
Oldham 22.11.1909   Lincoln 12.4.1982
23   4   (7.1936-5.1938)
Lancashire Schools, Birmingham ('28-30), Accrington ('30-31), Lincoln ('31-33), Notts County ('33-34), Cardiff ('34-36), Northampton ('36-38), Exeter ('38-39).
Division Three North championship medal with Lincoln, 1932.

RIOCH, Neil   Defender
Paddington 13.4.1951
14   4   (3.1972-4.1972 loan)
Luton ('68-69), Aston Villa ('69-75), York ('72 loan), Northampton ('72 loan), Plymouth ('75-77).
England Youth International. Brother to Bruce.

ROBERTS, Gordon   Winger
Foleshill 30.5.1925
70   13   (8.1944-3.1949)
Wolves (war), Northampton ('44-49), Brighton ('49-51), Accrington ('51-52), Cheltenham.
31 games and 12 goals for Northampton during the war.

ROBERTS, John   Goalkeeper
Cessnock (Australia) 24.3.1944
13   —   (7.1972-5.1973)
Chelsea ('66), Blackburn ('66-67), Chesterfield ('67-68), Bradford City ('68-71), Southend ('71-72), Northampton ('73-73).
Australian International.

John Roberts.

ROBERTS, John G.   Centre half
Swansea 11.9.1946
67   13   (11.1967-5.1969)
Swansea ('64-67), Northampton ('67-69), Arsenal ('69-72), Birminghamn ('72-76), Wrexham, ('76-80), Hull ('80-83).
Welsh International. Retired in 1983 through injury.

ROBERTSON, Stuart   Centre half
Nottingham 16.12.1946
280   28   (7.1972-5.1979)
Notts Forest ('64-66), Doncaster ('66-72), Northampton ('72-79), Bedford.
Now works in local leisure centre.

ROBINSON, Leslie St John   Inside forward
Romford 2.5.1898   Barking -.10.1968
79   38   (7.1925-7.1927)
West Ham United ('23-25), Northampton ('25-27), Norwich ('27-28).

ROBINSON, Maurice   Winger
Newark 9.11.1929
12   3   (6.1957-5.1958)
Leeds ('50), Gainsborough, Doncaster ('52-53), Kettering, Northampton ('57-58), Bedford.

ROBINSON, Terence   Defender
Woodhams 8.11.1929
14   —   (amateur)
Loughborough College, Brentford ('54-57), Northampton ('57-58), QPR ('58-59).
England Amateur International.

ROBINSON, Thomas   Forward
Coalville -.-.1909
7   2   (7.1935-5.1936)

Gresley Rovers, Birmingham ('29-30), Blackpool ('30-31), Chesterfield ('31-33), Lincoln ('33-35), Northampton ('35-36), Gillingham ('36-37).

ROBSON, Thomas   Defender
Morpeth -.-.1909
45   —   (8.1934-5.1938)
Everton ('32), Sheffield Wednesday ('30-32), Northampton (34-38), Kettering.

ROBSON, Tommy   Winger
Gateshead 3.7.1944
80 + 1   24   (8.1961-12.1965)
Northampton ('61-65), Chelsea ('65-66), Newcastle ('66-67), Peterborough ('67-79), Nuneaton, Stamford.
England Youth International. Most appearances for Peterborough, now Peterborough's youth team coach.

Colin Rodger. (G)

RODGER, Colin

RODGERS, Charles   Winger
Ayr
38   4   (3.1938-7.1939)
Ayr United, Manchester City ('34-37), Northampton ('37-39).
Represented Scottish League v Football League 1936.

ROE, James   Centre half
Local
1   —   (amateur)
Northampton ('20-21).

ROGERS, Eamon   Midfield
Dublin 16.4.1947
4   1   (12.1972 loan)
Blackburn ('65-71), Charlton ('71-72), Northampton ('72 loan), Eire International.

Eric Ross. (C&E)

ROSS, Eric   Midfield
Belfast 15.4.1943
65 + 7   5   (8.1969-10.1971)
Glentoran, Newcastle ('67-69), Northampton ('69-71), Hartlepool ('72 loan), Northern Ireland International.

ROSS, Ian   Defender
Glasgow 26.11.1947
2   —   (11.1976 loan)
Liverpool ('65-72), Aston Villa ('72-76), Notts County ('76-loan), Northampton ('76 loan), Peterborough ('76-79), Wolves ('79-80).

RUSSELL, Colin   Forward
7   8   (6.1931-6.1932)
Northampton ('31-32), Bournemouth ('32-33), Wolverton.

RUSSELL, George H.   Full back
Atherstone
55   —   (12.1927-6.1931)
Atherstone, Portsmouth ('19-20), Watford ('20-27), Northampton ('27-28), Atherstone, Cardiff ('28-31), Newport ('31-32), Stafford Rangers.

RUSSELL, Roger   Midfield
1964
1   —   (apprentice)

Syd Russell. (G)

RUSSELL, Sydney E. J.   Full back
Staines -.10.1911
117   —   (2.1936-4.1939)
Bradford   City   ('32-33),   QPR   ('33-35),
Northampton ('35-39).
Broke his leg v Southend 8.4.1939, and later
had it amputated.

Phil Sandercock.

SANDERCOCK, Phillip   Full back
Plymouth 21.6.1953
73   3   (9.1979-3.1981)
Torquay   ('71-77),   Huddersfield   ('77-79),
Northampton   ('79-81),   Nuneaton,
Wellingborough,   Barnet,   Weymouth,
Kettering.

SANDERS, Roy   Winger
London 22.9.1940
16   2   (5.1962-11.1962)
Romford, Northampton ('62), Romford.
Short stay at Northampton, mainly due to
injuries.

Adam Sandy. (PN)

SANDY, Adam Vincellete Cable   Midfield
Peterborough 22.9.1958
96 + 18   8   (12.1979-4.1983)
Kettering, Wolverton, Northampton ('79-83),
Wolverton, Wellingborough.
Emigrated to Australia for a spell; returned in
1987.

SANKEY, John   Wing half
Moulton, Norwich 19.3.1912   15.1.1985
52   —   (10.1945-5.1948)
Winsford, West Bromwich Albion ('37-45),
Northampton ('45-48), Hereford.
15 games and two goals for Northampton
during war. Joined Hereford as assistant
trainer/player; rejoined West Bromwich in
1954 as coach/scout.

Gary Sargent. (PN)

71

SARGENT, Gary Stewart Forward
Bedford 11.9.1952
49+2   4   (7.1979-12.1980)
Norwich City ('70-72), Scunthorpe ('72-74),
Bedford,   Peterborough   ('77-79),
Northampton   ('79-80),   Barnet,
Wellingborough, Irthlingborough Diamonds,
Spencer (player/manager).
Joined Cobblers in joint deal with Dennis
Byatt. Represented the FA v Cambridge
University. Now manager of local gymnasium.

SAUNDERS, Paul Utility
Watford 17.12.1959
130+14   5   (7.1978-5.1983)
Watford ('76-78), Northampton ('78-83),
Aylesbury.

Gary Saxby.

SAXBY, Gary Utility
Mansfield 11.12.1959
101+   13   (7.1980-5.1983)
Mansfield ('78-80), Northampton ('80-83),
Stafford Rangers.
Dropped into non-League football to become
a security guard.

SCHIAVI, Mark Winger
London 1.5.1964
35+5   6   (8.1985-10.1986)
West Ham United ('82-84), Bournemouth
('84-85), Northampton ('85-86), Cambridge
United (86-87), Kettering.
England Youth International. Member of
West Ham's winning Youth Cup side.

SCOTT, Christopher Defender
-+1   —   (8.1987-1.1988)
Cramlington, Whiley Bay, North Shields,
Blyth Spartans, Northampton ('87-88),
Darlington ('87 loan), Lincoln City.

SCOTT, Dave Goalkeeper
Belfast 6.6.1918
12   —   (10.1944-5.1948)
Northampton ('44-48), Headington.
11 wartime games for Northampton. Only
considered as cover, as part-time, preferring
to teach.

SCOTT, Geoff Defender
Birmingham 31.10.1956
21+3   —   (9.1984-5.1985)
Highgate, Stoke ('77-80), Leicester ('80-81),
Birmingham ('81-82), Charlton ('82-83),
Middlesbrough ('83-84), Northampton ('84-
85), Cambridge United ('85-86).

SCOTT, John Winger
Sunderland 5.2.1908
21   —   (8.1931-4.1932)
Dardon, Tempest, Colliery, Seaham Harbour,
Sunderland ('23-24), Darlington ('24-28),
Kettering,   Notts   Forest   ('29-31),
Northampton ('31-32), Exeter ('32-37),
Hartlepool ('37-38).

Arthur Seabrook.

SEABROOK, Arthur Forward
Luton
36   9   (7.1921-5.1924)
Luton Clarence, Northampton ('21-24),
Halifax ('24-28), Crewe ('28-29).

SEDDON, Sydney   Winger
Wellingborough
1   —   (cs1927-cs1928)
Rushden, Northampton ('27-28).

Steve Senior. (PN)

SENIOR, Steven   Full back
Sheffield 15.5.1963
2+4   —   (6.1987-11.1987)
York City ('81-87), Darlington ('86 loan),
Northampton ('87), Wigan ('88-).

Colin Sharpe. (C&E)

SHARPE, Colin   Full back
Bugbrooke -.-.1944
2   —   (cs1961-5.1965)
Northampton ('62-65), Kings Lynn.
County youth caps 1961, and Youth
International (England).

William Shaw.

SHAW, William W.   Inside left
Durham
80   14   (5.1925-6.1931)
Scarborough, Barcelona, Northampton ('25-
31).

SHIPLEY, A. G.   Wing half
1   —   (amateur)
Desborough,   Northampton   ('26-27),
Wellingborough, Rushden.

SHIRTLIFF, Paul   Midfield/defender
Barnsley 3.11.1962
28+2   —   (8.1984-5.1985)
Sheffield Wednesday ('79-84), Northampton
('84-85), Frickley.
England   semi-professional   International.
Brother to Peter, late of Sheffield Wednesday
and Charlton.

SIMONS, Reuben Rhys   Centre half
Swansea 16.10.1908
3   —   (5.1939-9.1939)
Swansea ('33-39), Northampton ('39).
Also made 12 wartime appearances for
Northampton.

SIMPSON, William   Left half
Cowdenbeath
44   —   (6.1936-5.1937)
Cowdenbeath   WMCA,   Musselburg
Brutonians, Foulford White Rose, Clyde,

Aston Villa ('32-36), Northampton ('36-37), Walsall ('37-39).

Martin Singleton. (PN)

SINGLETON, Martin

Albert Sissons.

SISSONS, Albert Edward   Winger
Kiverton Park 5.7.1903   Birmingham 1975
21   5   (6.1929-6.1930)
Doncaster ('23-25), Leeds ('25-28), Southport
('28-29), Northampton ('29-30).

SKEET, Stuart   Goalkeeper
Cheshunt 6.7.1948
1   —   (4.1969 loan)
Tottenham ('65-69), Northampton ('69).
First loan player at Northampton.

Trevor Slack. (PN)

SLACK, Trevor

Tom Smalley.

SMALLEY, Thomas   Full back
Kinsley, Yorks 13.1.1912   1.4.1984
226   2   (10.1941-5.1951)
South Kirkby Colliery, Wolves ('32-38),
Norwich ('38-41), Northampton ('41-51),
Lower Gornal (player/coach).
England International (one cap); 201 wartime
appearances for Northampton and 12 goals.
Also guested for WBA during the war.

A. Smith. (G)

SMITH, A.   Centre half
Northampton
1   —   (5.1938-5.1939)
Northampton ('38-39).

Harry Smith. (C&E)

SMITH, Charles Harry   Goalkeeper
Small Heath
181   —   (9.1913-5.1926)
Coventry ('10-12), Northampton ('12-26),
Higham.
Also made 14 appearances in the Southern
League.

Dave Smith. (C&E)

SMITH, David   Inside forward
Durham 12.10.1915
141   13   (3.1946-4.1951)
South   Shields,   Newcastle   ('38-39),
Northampton ('46-51).
Ten wartime appearances and one goal for
Northampton.
Also played for the Rhine Army in Germany.
In 1951 became the Club secretary; took over
as manager in 1955; became Aldershot's
manager in 1959; later returned to Derby (for
whom he guested during the war), to run a
newsagents.

SMITH,
  Eddie W. A. (Ginger)   Inside forward
London 23.3.1929
56   13   (1.1955-5.1956)
Wealdstone, Bournemouth ('48-50), Chelsea
('50-53), Watford ('53-55), Northampton ('55-
56), Colchester ('56-57), QPR ('57-58).
Always part-time at Northampton, running a
newsagents in London.

SMITH, H. Ray   Inside forward
Hull 13.9.1934
24   8   (10.1962-10.1963)
Hereford, Portsmouth ('50-52), Hull ('52-60),
Peterborough ('60-62), Northampton ('62-
63), Luton ('63-64).

Jack Smith. (C&E)

SMITH, Jack O.   Wing half
Whetstone, Leicester 4.9.1928
197   9   (9.1949-6.1960)
Leicester (amateur), Northampton ('49-60).
Granted a benefit v Peterborough April 1956.
Appeared as wicket-keeper for Northants'
second eleven in the '50s.

SMITH, Tom Gable   Inside forward
Whitburn, Sunderland   Whitburn
-.10.1900   21.2.1934
122   22   (8.1927-5.1930)
Leicester ('21-23), Manchester United ('23-
26), Northampton ('26-30), Norwich ('30-31).

SMITH, William H.   Forward
Durham 7.9.1926
28   8   (7.1948-2.1959)
Plymouth United, Plymouth Argyle ('45-47),
Reading ('47-48), Northampton ('48-50),
Birmingham ('50-52), Blackburn ('52-60),
Accrington ('60-61 player/coach).

SORENSON, I.   Winger
Northampton
1   —   (Amateur)
Northampton Nomads, Northampton ('23-
24).

Jack Southam. (C&E)

SOUTHAM, James H. (Jack)   Full back
Willenhall 19.8.1917
154   1   (6.1949-5.1955)
Shornhill Recreation WBA (war), Newport
('46), Birmingham ('46-49), Norwich ('49-55),
Walsall (assistant trainer/player).
Guested for Arsenal, Ipswich, Newport.
Missed out on a testimonial with
Northampton, due to the length of his last
season, when the Club was unable to arrange
a match.

SPELMAN, Ron   Winger
Bloefield, Norfolk 22.5.1938
37   3   (11.1960-2.1962)
CNDSBU, Norwich ('56-60), Northampton
('60-62), Bournemouth ('62-63), Watford ('63-
65), Oxford ('65-67), Wisbech, Bletchley
United.
Moved to Bournemouth in exchange for
Woollard.

SPROSTON, Arthur   Full back
7   1   (Amateur)
Northampton ('19-21), Desborough.
40 Southern League appearances for
Northampton.

STANTON, Sidney   Defender
Dudley 16.6.1923
7   —   (7.1946-7.1948)
Birmingham ('45-46), Northampton ('46-49).

Alan Starling. (C&E)

STARLING, Alan (Sparrow)   Goalkeeper
Barking 2.4.1951
258   1   (7.1971-2.1977)
Luton ('68-71), Torquay ('71 loan),
Northampton ('71-77), Huddersfield ('77-81),
Bradford City ('81 non-contract).
Originally signed on loan for Northampton.
Only 'keeper to score for the Club in a League
game, when he converted a penalty v
Hartlepool in 1976.

STAROSCIK, Felix   Winger
Silesia, Poland 20.5.1920

50 19 (7.1951-5.1955)
Wolves (amateur), Third Lanark, Northampton ('51-55), Bedford.

STRANG, Richard Centre half
Rutherglen
7 — (6.1932-6.1933)
Scottish Junior Football, Birmingham ('24-26), Crystal Palace ('25-27), Poole, Halifax ('29-32), Northampton ('32-33), Darlington ('33-36).

Paul Stratford. (C&E)

STRATFORD, Paul Forward
Northampton 4.9.1955
184 + 3 60 (10.1972-6.1978)
Northampton ('72-78)
Retired through injury. Granted testimonial, April 1980.

STRATHIE, James W. Defender
Beancross 12.2.1913 1976
9 — (6.1939-6.1947)
St Bernards, Luton ('37-39), Northampton ('39-47), Corby Town.

SUGRUE, Paul Forward
Coventry 6.11.1960
2 + 7 2 (3.1986-9.1986)
Nuneaton, Manchester City ('79-80), Cardiff ('81-83), Kansas, Middlesbrough ('82-84), Portsmouth ('85-86), Northampton ('86), Newport ('86-88), Bridgend.

SYRETT, David K. Forward
Salisbury 20.1.1956
50 + 2 17 (8.1982-3.1984)
Swindon ('73-77), Mansfield ('77-79), Wolves ('78 loan), Walsall ('79), Peterborough ('79-82), Northampton ('82-84), Brackley.
Retired through back injury; became a milkman in Towcester.

TAYLOR, Andrew Full back
Stratford-on-Avon -.-.62

22 — (7.1981-5.1982)
Aston Villa ('79-81), Northampton ('81-82), A. P. Leamington, Alvechurch.

TAYLOR, Anthony Defender
Glasgow 6.9.1946
6 + 1 — (6.1979-10.1979)
Kilmarnock, Celtic, Morton, Crystal Palace ('68-74), Southend ('74-76), Swindon ('76-77), Bristol Rovers ('77-78), Portsmouth ('78-79), Northampton ('79 player/coach).

TAYLOR, J. Defender
1 — (6.1930-7.1931)
Northampton ('30-31)

TEBBUTT, Robert Inside forward
Irchester 10.11.1934
59 22 (10.1956-10.1960)
Northampton ('56-60), Bedford, Kettering.
County youth player ('53). Suffered broken leg v Walsall 1960, which ended League career.

TERRY, Patrick Centre forward
Lambeth 2.10.1933
28 11 (7.1961-1.1962)
Eastbourne, Charlton ('54-56), Newport ('56-58), Swansea ('58).
Gillingham ('58-61), Northampton ('61-62), Millwall ('62-64), Reading ('64-67), Swindon ('67-68), Brentford ('68-69), Hillingdon Borough, Wimbledon, Folkestone.

Bill Thayne. (G)

THAYNE, William   Centre half
West Hartlepool -.-.1912   -.7.1986
138   —   (3.1936-6.1939)
Crystal Palace ('29), Hartlepool ('29-35), Luton ('35-36), Northampton ('36-39), Walsall ('39-40).
Local boxer in Hartlepool. Guested for Birmingham during war.

THOMAS, William D.   Inside forward
21   2   (2.1950-5.1921)
Northampton ('20-21).
Also made eight appearances, and scored two goals for the Club in the Southern League.

THOMPSON, Harry   Wing half
Mansfield 29.4.1915
45   3   (11.1946-5.1949)
Mansfield ('35-37), Wolves ('37-38), Sunderland ('38-39), York ('39-46), Northampton ('46-49), Headington ('49-56 player/manager).

THOMPSON, Keith   Forward
Birmingham 24.4.1965
10   1   (3.1985-4.1985 loan)
Coventry ('83-85), Wimbledon ('84 loan), Northampton ('85 loan), Portuguese football. Brother of Gary Thompson.

THOMPSON, Walter   Full back
Sheffield -.-.1911
2   —   (1.1933-6.1934)
Aston Villa ('31-33), Northampton ('33-34), Scarborough.

THOMPSON, William S.   Full back
7   —   (7.1934-7.1936)
Wellingborough, Northampton ('34-36).

THORPE, Thomas   Goalkeeper
Kinhurst, Sheffield 19.5.1881   28.9.1953
40   —   (9.1909-5.1921)
Doncaster ('01-05), Barnsley ('05-09), Northampton ('09-21), Barnsley ('21-22).
Also made 253 Southern League appearances, and converted two penalties. Made three appearances for the Northants County cricket team in 1913, as a middle order batsman.

Fred Tilsom.

TILSOM, Samuel Frederick   Forward
Barnsley 19.4.1904   Manchester 21.11.1972
42   11   (3.1938-5.1939)
Regent St Cones, Barnsley ('26-28), Manchester City ('28-38), Northampton ('38-39), York ('39-40).
England International. FA Cup winners' medal with Manchester City, 1934. Part of the three man deal that came from City in exchange for Dunkley.

TOLLAND, Daniel   Forward
Scotland -.-.1905
161   30   (6.1933-12.1937)
Ayr United, Northampton ('33-37), Bristol Rovers ('37-39).
Emigrated to USA.

TOMKINS, Eric Felthan   Wing half
Rushden 18.12.1892   Rushden 20.7.1980
91   1   (9.1911-5.1923)
Northampton ('11-23), Rushden.
England schoolboy International, captained first-ever side. Made 149 appearances for Club in Southern League. 13 matches for the County cricket side 1913, as right-handed bat. Guested for Tottenham during World War I.

TOWNSEND, Neil   Centre half
Long Buckby 1.2.1950
69 + 3   2   (3.1968-7.1973)
Northampton ('68-72), Southend ('72-78),
Weymouth, Bournemouth ('79-80).
County youth player. England Youth
International (1968).

TOWNSEND, Russell   Midfield
Reading 17.1.1960
14 + 1   —   (9.1979-3.1980)
Arsenal (apprentice), Barnet, Northampton
('79-80), Barnet.

Ray Train.

TRAIN, Ray   Midfield
Nuneaton 10.2.1951
54   3   (7.1984-5.1985)
Walsall ('68-71), Carlisle ('71-76), Sunderland
('76-77), Bolton ('77-78), Watford ('78-81),
Oxford ('81-84), Bournemouth ('84 loan),
Northampton ('84-85), Tranmere ('85-86),
Walsall ('86 player/coach).
Combined transfer fees, over £200,000. Came
to Northampton at end of '83-84 season on
loan, but did not play, due to injury.

Jack Tresadern.

TRESADERN, John   Inside forward
Leytonstone   Tonbridge
26.9.1890   26.12.1959
33   1 (6.1925-12.1926 as player)
Barking, West Ham United ('13-14), Burnley
('24-25), Northampton ('25-27).
England International, two caps. FA Cup
winners' medal with West Ham United 1923.
Managerial career: Crystal Palace ('30-35),
Tottenham ('35-38), Plymouth ('38-47), Aston
Villa ('48-49), Chelmsford ('49-50), Hastings
('50-51), Tonbridge ('58-59).

Barry Tucker. (C&E)

TUCKER, Barry   Full back
Swansea 28.8.1952
295 + 6   8   (9.1970-2.1978)
                      (10.1982-5.1984)
Northampton ('71-78), Brentford ('78-82),
Northampton ('82-84).

TUCKER, Kenneth J.   Winger
Merthyr Tydfil 15.7.1935
14   3   (3.1960-5.1961)
Merthyr Tydfil, Aston Villa (amateur), Cardiff ('55-58), Shrewsbury ('58-60), Northampton ('60-61), Hereford ('61-63), Merthyr Tydfil.
Later became the Merthyr secretary.

TUMBRIDGE, Raymond   Full back
London 6.3.1955
11   —   (2.1975-4.1975 loan)
Charlton ('73-75), Northampton ('75 loan). Cheltenham, Dartford, Gravesend.
Will be remembered as the first Northampton player to sport a beard.

TURNER, George   Winger
—
23   3   (3.1936-6.1937)
Notts County ('29-31), Luton ('31-32), Everton ('32), Bradford City ('32-35), Luton ('35-36), Northampton ('36-37).

TYSOE, Frank   Defender
—
1   —   (amateur)
Northampton ('19-22).

UPTON, Frank   Wing half
Nuneaton 18.10.1934
17   1   (3.1953-5.1954)
Nuneaton, Northampton ('53-54), Derby ('54-61), Chelsea ('61-65), Derby ('65-66), Notts County ('66-67), Worcester, Workington (player/manager).
When he moved to Northampton, Nuneaton received a fee plus two players in exchange for the rest of the season. Returned to Northampton as coach/scout in 1970 for three months. Aston Villa third team coach; assistant manager at Chelsea, and manager for 24 hours. Managed Feta of Denmark; scout to Derby.

VICKERS, Peter   Inside forward
Doncaster 6.3.1934
2   —   (1.1960-5.1960)
Leeds ('52-54), March Town, Kings Lynn, Wisbech, Lincoln ('59), Northampton ('59-60).
England schoolboy International.

WAINWRIGHT, Robin   Midfield
Luton 9.3.1951
26 + 9   5   (2.1974-3.1974 loan)
                      (7.1974-3.1975)

Luton ('68-72), Millwall ('72-74), Cambridge United ('73 loan), Northampton ('74-75), Milton Keynes, Ampthill Town, Dunstable, Hillingdon Borough, Wealdstone.

'Fanny' Walden.

WALDEN,
   Fredrick Ingram (Fanny)   Winger
Wellingborough   Northampton
1.3.1888   3.5.1949
21   1   (10.1909-7.1913)
                      (6.1926-5.1927)
Wellingborough, Northampton ('09-13), Tottenham ('13-26), Northampton ('26-27).
England International. Division two championship with Tottenham, 1920. Scored hat-trick on Cobblers' debut, at centre forward, despite being only 5 feet 1 inch. Played for County, right-hand batsman, slow bowler, centre point fielder; with W. W. Timms, set up a seventh wicket stand of 229 for Northants; later became a first class umpire.

Harry Walden. (C&E)

WALDEN, Harry   Winger
Walgrave 22.12.1940
85   4   (6.1964-6.1967)
Kettering, Luton ('61-64), Northampton ('64-67), Kettering.
Joined in an exchange deal with Billy Hails, who moved to Luton.

Des Waldock. (C&E)

WALDOCK, Desmond   Defender
Northampton 4.12.1961
59 + 2   4   (12.1978-6.1981)
Long Buckby, Northampton ('78-81), Banbury, Long Buckby.
County youth player, 1978.

Clive Walker. (PN)

WALKER, David Clive   Full back
Watford 24.10.1945
80   1   (10.1966-7.1969)
Leicester ('62-66), Northampton ('66-69), Mansfield ('69-75), Chelmsford, Gravesend.
England schoolboy International. Has held several positions since returning to Northampton: youth team coach, coach and manager.

WALKER, Ricky   Full back
Northampton 4.4.1959
57 + 4   —   (8.1978-6.1981)
Coventry ('77-78), Northampton ('78-81), Corby, Valley Sports Rugby.

WALLACE, James   Centre half
Kirkintilloch 17.2.1933
1   —   (6.1955-6.1956)
Aberdeen, Northampton ('55-56), Aberdeen.

WALLBANK, Fredrick   Forward
Wigan -.-.1911
1   —   (7.1936-5.1937)
Bury ('27-28) Chesterfield ('28-29), Bradford City ('31-32), West Ham United ('32-35), Notts Forest ('35-36), Northampton ('36-37).
Brother of James, who played for the Club four seasons earlier; one of five footballing brothers.

WALLBANK, James   Defender
Wigan 12.9.1909   Reading 28.10.1979
2   —   (cs1932-cs1933)
Barnsley   ('29-31),   Norwich   ('31-32),

Northampton ('32-33), Bradford City ('34-35), Millwall ('35-36), Reading ('46).

WALSH, William   Centre half
Durham 4.12.1923
19   —   (7.1953-6.1954)
Sunderland ('46-53), Northampton ('53-54), Darlington ('54-55).
Bought for £6,000, together with Maurice Maston.

WALTON, Ronald   Winger
Plymouth 12.10.1945
1   —   (9.1963-10.1965)
Rotherham ('62-63), Northampton ('63-65), Crewe ('65-66), Carlisle ('66), Aldershot ('66-71), Cambridge United ('71-73), Aldershot ('73-76), Dartford, Blyth Spartans, Hampton.

WARD, Richard   Inside forward
Scunthorpe 16.9.1940
6   —   (amateur)
Scunthorpe Grammar School, Scunthorpe ('58-59), Northampton ('59-60), Tooting and Mitcham, Millwall ('62-63).

WARD, Robert   Goalkeeper
West Bromwich 4.8.1953
8   —   (2.1977-3.1977 loan)
West Bromwich Albion ('73-77), Northampton ('77 loan), Blackpool ('77-79), Wigan ('79-82).

WARD, Stephen   Midfield
Brighton 21.7.1959
17 + 2   3   (6.1979-2.1980)
Brighton ('77-79), Northampton ('79-80), Halifax ('80-86), Kettering.

WARREN, Ernest   Forward
Sunderland 14.9.1910
3   1   (7.1933-7.1934)
Udsworth, Southampton ('30-31), Burton Town, Northampton ('33-34), Hartlepool ('34-35).

WASSELL, Kim   Utility
Birmingham 9.6.1957
14 + 9   —   (9.1977-5.1979)
West Bromwich Albion ('75-77), Northampton ('77-79), Aldershot ('79-80), Hull ('83-84), Swansea ('84-85), Wolves ('85-86).

Bill Watson.

WATSON, William   Full back
Carlisle
312   4   (8.1920-6.1929)
Carlisle, Northampton ('20-29).

J. Watson.

WATSON, William James B.   Forward
—
18   4   (8.1934-5.1935)
Tunbridge Wells, Bristol Rovers ('33-34), Northampton ('34-35), Gillingham.

WATTS, Derek   Full back
Leicester 30.6.1952
— + 1   —   (10.1973 loan)
Leicester ('70-74), Northampton ('73 loan), Torquay ('74-76).

WEAVER, Eric Winger
Rhymney 1.7.1943
69 + 2   9   (12.1967-6.1970)
Trowbridge, Swindon ('62-67), Notts County ('67), Northampton ('67-70), Boston, Hereford.

WEBBER, George Goalkeeper
Cardiff 26.6.1925
13   —   (6.1954-6.1955)
Cardiff ('48-50), Torquay ('50-54), Northampton ('54-55), Ebbw Vale.

Tommy Wells.

WELLS, Thomas C. Winger
Nunhead
307   85   (2.1927-5.1935)
Arsenal ('23-27), Northampton ('27-35), Swindon ('35-36), Orient ('36-37).

WESTON, C. A. Winger
Kettering
4   —   (10.1920-5.1922)
Kettering Atlas, Northampton ('20-21).

John Weston.

WESTON, John Matthew Winger
Halesowen
46   16   (5.1928-5.1932)
Burnley ('27-28), Northampton ('28-32).

WHEELER, Alfred Forward
Bilston
5   1   (7.1933-5.1934)
Walsall ('31-32), Brentford ('32-33), Northampton ('33-34), Southampton ('34-35), Gillingham.

George Whitworth.

WHITWORTH,
  George H. (Twitty) Forward
Northampton 14.7.1896
75   46   (8.1914-2.1922)
Rushden Windmill, Northampton ('14-22), Crystal Palace ('22-26), Sheffield Wednesday ('26), Hull ('26-28), South Shields.
Made 53 appearances and 30 goals in the Southern League. Guested for Crystal Palace during First World War; later ran a fish and chip shop in South Shields.

WHYTE, Campbell Winger
Lochyelly
5   1   (8.1930-5.1931)
Cowdenbeath, Third Lanark, Gillingham, Northampton ('30-31), Arbroath, Rochdale ('33-34).

Russell Wilcox. (PN)

WILCOX, Russell (Ronnie)

WILLIAMS, Brett   Full back
Dudley 19.3.1968
4 + 1   —   (1.1988-2.1988 loan)
Notts Forest ('85-), Stockport ('87 loan),
Northampton ('88 loan).

WILLIAMS, Edgar   Goalkeeper
Sheffield 20.5.1919
3   —   (6.1948-6.1949)
Rotherham ('46-47), Notts Forest ('47-48),
Northampton ('48-49).

WILLIAMS, J. E.   Defender
Rugby
2   —   (amateur)
Rugby, Northampton ('21-22).

Keith Williams.

WILLIAMS, Keith   Midfield
Burntwood 12.4.1957
137 + 4   7   (2.1977-6.1981)
Aston Villa ('75-77), Northampton ('77-81),
Bournemouth ('81-87 player/coach), Bath ('87
loan), Colchester ('87 player/coach).

WILLIAMS, Roland   Forward
Swansea 10.7.1927
15   —   (3.1956-11.1957)

WILLIAMS, William   Wing half
Cardiff
198   4   (7.1921-7.1927)
Cardiff ('19-21), Northampton ('21-27),
Newport ('27-28).
Welsh International (one cap).

WILSON, F.   Wing half
Kettering
1   —   (5.1926-5.1927)
Rothwell, Northampton ('26-27).

WILSON, James   Full back
Musselburgh 28.6.1922
24   —   (7.1951-9.1954)
Musselburgh, Durbar, Peterborough, Luton
('50-51), Northampton ('51-53), Chesterfield
('53-54).
Represented the RAF.

WILSON, John R.   Wing half
Blyth
16   1   (8.1927-5.1928)
Portsmouth ('25-26), Reading ('26-27),
Northampton ('27-28).

WILSON, Paul

WILSON, Samuel   Forward
Glasgow 16.12.1931
1   1   (7.1960-7.1961)
St Mirren, Celtic, Millwall ('58-60),

WOAN, Alan   Forward
Liverpool 8.2.1931
124   70   (7.1956-10.1959)
New Brighton, Norwich ('53-56),
Northampton ('56-59), Crystal Palace ('59-61),
Aldershot ('61-64), Chertsey.
Scored the first goal in the Fourth Division for
Northampton v Port Vale, in the first minute
of the game.

WONNACOTT,
  Clarence Benjamin   Forward
Clowne, Derby, 31.12.1909
13   4   (8.1930-5.1932)
Mansfield ('28-30), Northampton ('30-32),
Shelbourne, Mansfield ('33-34).

WOOD, Alfred D.   Goalkeeper
Birmingham 14.5.1915
146   —   (12.1951-5.1955)
Sutton Ashfield, Nuneaton, Coventry ('37-51), Northampton ('51-55), Coventry ('55-59 player/coach).
91 wartime games for Northampton, also guested for Mansfield, Chesterfield, Coventry and Derby. Oldest player for the Cobblers, just two weeks off his 40th birthday when he played his last game in 1955. Returned to Coventry as coach and was forced into playing due to injuries. Later had a spell as Walsall's manager.

WOOD, Edmund Eli   Centre half
Kings Norton, 10.2.1903
51   3   (3.1923-5.1925)
Redditch, Rhyl, Northampton ('22-25), Birmingham ('25-26), Rhyl, Newcastle ('28-30), Rhyl.

WOOD, John T.   Utility
Local 1902
1   —   (5.1921-5.1922)
Daventry, Northampton ('21-22).

WOOD, William   Forward
Parkgate, Rotherham -.-.1900
37   9   (7.1923-7.1924)
Oldham ('19-23), Northampton ('23-24), Swansea ('24-26), Wellingborough.

WOODS, Derek   Winger
Northampton 23.3.1941
6   2   (amateur)
England Amateur International

Arnold Woollard. (C&E)

WOOLLARD, Arnold   Full back
24.8.1930
Bermuda
34   —   (6.1949-12.1952)
                   (3.1962-6.1963)
Hamilton Bermuda, Bermuda Amateur Athletic, Northampton ('50-52), Peterborough, Newcastle ('52-56), Bournemouth ('56-62), Northampton ('62-63).
Two spells at Northampton, second one in exchange for Ron Spelman. Returned to Bermuda to work in local government.

WOOLETT, Alan H.   Defender
Leicester 4.3.1947
28   —   (7.1978-5.1979)
Leicester ('68-78), Northampton ('78-79), Corby.

WRIGHT, Michael   Forward
Newmarket 16.1.1942
27   7   (11.1959-5.1961)
Newmarket, Northampton ('59-61), Kings Lynn.
Made over 1,000 appearances for Kings Lynn.

WRIGHT, R.   Forward
Kettering
1   —   (amateur)
Northampton Amateurs, Northampton ('23-24).

YEOMANS, Rae   Wing half
Perth 13.5.1934
175   7   (6.1953-10.1958)
St Johnstone, Northampton ('53-59), Middlesbrough ('59-68), Darlington ('68-70) (player/manager).
Only player that Bob Dennison took with him to Middlesbrough. Later became youth team coach to both Sunderland and Middlesbrough; also scouted for Northampton in mid-'70s.

YORK, Rowland   Forward
—
3   —   (8.1923-5.1924)
Kettering, Fletton, Higham, Northampton ('23-24).

YORKE, Andrew   Full back
Blyth, Northumberland -.-.1901
24   —   (8.1925-6.1927)
Blyth Spartans, Sunderland ('21-23), Coventry ('23-25), Northampton ('25-27), Lincoln ('27-28).

ABOVE: 1938-39 team. BELOW: 1949-50 team. (C&E)

I REMEMBER

A selection of players, from the Second World War until a few seasons ago, relive their days at the County ground. Some are happy, some sad, some humorous, but all keep a place in their hearts for Northampton Town. The players' memories are recorded in chronological order.

Jack Jennings

My first contact with Northampton Town was during the war. I had played First Division football from the age of 17 with Cardiff prior to the war; then, when I joined the Army, I was posted to Bedford, where I was asked by the Cobblers' manager, Tom Smith, to be a 'guest' player for the Club. This I did and, when I was demobbed, I became the trainer/coach. I assisted in building a team to get out of the Third Division South and, as a qualified physiotherapist, I treated all the injuries.

They were a happy bunch of lads that gathered in my treatment room after a match, to hear the football results, and most of them came in again on a Sunday morning for treatment, bringing their children with them. Lads who had been injured in the local park matches also turned up; all were welcome. It was more like a social club than a football club, sometimes.

One very happy memory was when we beat Arsenal in the FA Cup, a real red letter day for the Club. Another great honour was, while at Northampton, to be appointed trainer/coach/physio to the England Amateur team, a position I held for 25 years, covering 250 games and three Olympics.

My greatest ambition was to see the Club in a higher division, and this great moment came when we were promoted from the Third Division.

We were fortunate to sign several England amateur players who were turning professional, like Laurie Brown, Bobby Brown and Peter Kane; they were a great help in our rise. A special memory was my benefit match; several players I had played against in the pre-war days, including Stanley Matthews, came, and the Chief Constable informed me that all the police, many of whom I had treated, gave their services free that day.

I also enjoyed coaching the Oxford University side, Wellingborough School and Great Houghton School, as well as giving many talks and lectures to different clubs. It was through my wife that we signed Roly Mills, and she actually came along to the signing.

Bobby King

My earliest memory of my Northampton days goes back to November 1937, when I left my Far Cotton home to watch the Cobblers play Cardiff in an FA Cup tie. At the time I had just won a place in the reserve side, so it was some surprise to arrive at the ground and to be told by the manager, 'Get undressed, you're playing'. Although we lost 1-2, it will be a game I will always remember.

I had joined the Club as a professional a month earlier, and exactly two years later I was drafted into the RAF, where I stayed until March 1946.

I did make a bit of history, by being the first player to be transferred during the war, when I signed for Wolves. Christmas 1947 I was back in Northampton, having been signed to replace Archie Garrett, who had joined Birmingham. As I travelled down to Northampton by train I would often bump into Archie, who would be waiting for his train to Birmingham. On retiring from the game I joined the Electricity Board. I remember playing in the pre-war side in the youngest forward line ever: myself, Harry Jennings, Eli Hurrell, Dick Ellwood and Bill Barron.

Bill Barron

Whenever I think of my playing days I always think of the 1946/47 season. We had drawn Preston North End in the third round of the FA Cup. In those days they were a First Division outfit and had several Internationals, and my job was to mark one of these — Tom Finney.

For a few days before, and up to the time of the kick-off, I felt a bit excited and rather nervous, thinking that he might give me the run-around.

Although we lost the game 1-2, it was one of the best I ever had for the Cobblers. Once the match had started I lost all my nervousness, and through the whole game more than held my own. It was an honour to have played against such a great player.

Tommy Fowler

There are quite a few memories in my stay at the County Ground, but two in particular stand out in my mind. The first was our trip to Liverpool, in the FA Cup match during the 1957/58 season. I was born about eight miles from the Anfield ground and, as a schoolboy, I was a regular visitor to see Liverpool play, my home being Prescott, a small town in those days. It was quite a thrill for me to play there, especially in the Cup. We were a large family, so all my relatives were there, including my father, plus a great many people from Prescott. I remember the Club took us to Southport on the Tuesday before the game; we had four memorable days' training there, with three to four inches of snow lying about.

My second memory was playing my 500th game for the Club. Frank Jenner, the then secretary, took me into town to a jewellers to select a gold watch; Frank himself presented it to me on the pitch at the next home game.

There was also one very funny incident that involved my wife. She was travelling home by 'bus after a home match (no car then), and I had not had a very good game. Two gentlemen sat at the front and they gave me hell, from the County Ground, to the bottom of Abington Street. As she alighted my wife said to one of them 'You know, he has been in bed all week with 'flu'. The gentleman replied 'And what do you know about it', or words to that effect. 'Well,' she retorted, 'I ought to, I've been getting in and out of bed with him for the last five or six years', and then got off the 'bus.

A few days later, the *Chronicle & Echo*, in the column headed 'Hamptune', ran a piece called 'My most embarrassing moment', and one of the gentlemen proceeded to relate the story.

Gwyn Hughes

My most memorable occasion was being picked to represent the Third Division South v the Third Division North in the very first encounter between the two Leagues.

I was disappointed to be told before the match that I was to be substituted at half time; unfortunately for me, the second half was to be televised, and all my friends in Wales had made arrangements to watch the game — no mean feat as there were few TVs in Wales at the time since reception was so poor.

The day I remember most was an FA Cup replay at Southampton in January 1950; we travelled down by coach and the sight of thousands of supporters on the way was something to behold. Every country pub we passed had a coachload of supporters outside, wavng their scarves as we went by; they started as early as the Green Man at Syresham.

Of the players I played with, two of the bravest were Arthur Dixon and Jack English. They were both slightly built but as brave as they come. I can see Arthur now, laid out as he scored the first goal against Derby in a fifth round FA Cup tie. The way Jack used to take on opposing defenders and score all those goals so coolly was magic. For all-round ability and contribution, I must mention Tommy Fowler, so good for so long.

Maurice Candlin

Northampton was a very friendly club; all the players worked as a team, and individuality was moulded into overall teamwork. Players for the most part were determined to win, and there were few passengers, if any. The game against Arsenal that we lost 3-2 will always be in the forefront of my memory. We were somewhat unlucky to lose and many of the Arsenal supporters asked why Northampton were in the Third Division.

Of the players that impressed me, I must mention Tommy Fowler, one of the quickest wing players in any side; Tom Smalley, with his extremely positive attitude to the game — 'We are going to win'; Adam McCulloch, another 100% man, very pleasant to know and easy to get along with (we were together at Partick Thistle); Jack English, a good footballer with good control, and most important, he could score goals, and Jack Ansell, with his tremendous agility in keeping the ball out of the net.

It wasn't unknown to play in front of big crowds in my days, 20,000-30,000; I can understand players of today being unable to motivate themselves with such small crowds. I also note a lack of discipline from players and officials throughout the game today — so many decisions are questioned.

The worst feature of British football today is lack of crowd discipline; we did not see much of it in my playing days, but I suppose it was simmering below the surface. Again, I feel lack of discipline on the field causes a lot of crowd disturbance.

I also wonder how players today would get on with the old leather ball; when it became wet, it became harder to kick, and some thought twice about heading it (I didn't hesitate, but those without brains generally didn't).

Freddie Ramscar

The first season I ever played for Northampton was my best season; I played in 52 games, was ever-present, and netted 28 times. I took all the penalties, as I did in all of my stay at Northampton. We scored more goals than any other Club in the League. I also created a record I was not aware of, scoring in every game for nine weeks running.

Joe Payne

As a player with Swansea, Newport and Scunthorpe, prior to joining Northampton in August 1951, I experienced many memorable occasions. The most memorable at the County ground was the hat-trick I scored for the Cobblers; all three were in 19 minutes of the first half and against one of my old clubs, Newport.

Another wonderful occasion was as senior trainer/coach in 1964, when we won promotion to the First Division, after the great 4-1 win at Bury. It assured us of participating in the cream of English soccer.

Don Adams

Being locally born, and overlooking the Cobblers ground, stimulated my enthusiasm to be a professional footballer, at a very early age. I spent many hours as a boy, in the ground, not only at matches but also at training sessions, and can recall many respected players and teams of the time.

As a youth I played for the local Boys Brigade team (6th BBOB). I sustained an ankle injury — damaged ligaments — and our neighbour at the time was deputy groundsman, Jack Mason; he suggested I call in and see Jack Jennings. In general conversation with Jack, who had Tommy Mulgrew under treatment at the time, I explained I was on amateur forms with Chelsea, so he suggested I had a trial with Northampton when I was fit.

From this opportunity I progressed most happily through the 'A' team, the reserves (who often drew crowds of 6,000), to eventually play my first Division Three South match for the Club as a professional v Plymouth Argyle. I had best wishes telegrams from many people, including one from my old Boys Brigade side, which I greatly treasure.

One memorable game in Division Three South at Leyton Orient I will never forget. I left the field after five minutes to have two stitches over my right eye. Jack English joined me in the dressing room a few minutes later with a dislocated collar bone, and at half time Ron Patterson was concussed by a home supporter hitting him over the head with a bottle.

I returned to the field in the second half, after treatment, to make up a nine man side (no subs in those days), and in another five minutes I clashed with the home centre, Bill Aldous, getting a damaged knee; this time I was out of the game. We managed to hold out for a draw against a team who, like us, were in contention for top place. Strange as it appears, it was not a dirty game.

My career, on reflection, was unfortunately dogged with similar injuries every time I settled into the first team.

Reg Elvy

During my short stay with the Cobblers the two most vivid memories are the Cup games in 1958 against Arsenal and Liverpool.

The Arsenal game was at the County ground and we won 3-1; this put us in the fourth round and we drew Liverpool, away.

Having played at Anfield a number of times for both Blackburn and Bolton, it was old stamping ground for me. The things that stood out in that game were terrible weather conditions (across the city, the Everton game had been cancelled), and the fact that we lost. The turning point in the game came through the brilliant own goal scored by dear old Ben Collins, who incidentally could not be blamed in any way; however these things happen in football, and you soon learn to forget them.

It was good experience for the Club and supporters, who still like to stop and talk about it today.

Ben Collins

Looking back over the 13 years I spent at the County Ground, three games stand out most in my mind.

1950: Playing against Notts County at Meadow Lane and marking my school boy hero, Tommy Lawton. This match was played in the evening during the mid-week. A crowd of over 31,000 enjoyed a thrilling game, the home side winning 2-0 and winning promotion from the old Third Division South.

In 1958: One of the greatest matches at the County ground in the history of the club — Northampton 3 Arsenal 1. Over 21,000 crowded to see us make this memorable day. TV cameras filmed the game for Match-of-the-day, the first time cameras had ever visited the County Ground. For that game we were all given a free pair of shoes that a Mansfield shoe company donated.

The next round for us was the fourth round at Liverpool. Prior to this game we spent a week of special training at Southport (it snowed most of the week).

In front of a crowd of 57,000, with the ground in atrocious conditions, we settled down well, with the score at 1-1; I scored at the famous Kop end, to make it 2-1 — alas the wrong end: it was an own goal. The match ended 3-1 to the famous Anfield team.

One of my favourite stories concerns visiting the Dell at Southampton to play a cup match replay, a game we won 3-2 (1950).

Fourteen players made up the squad and three of us that did not play shared a bonus of £2 between us — thirteen shillings and fourpence each (67p). My wages were £7 in the winter and £5 in the summer (some thought we were still overpaid).

Roly Mills

Of all the 324 appearances I made during my career, my most vivid memories are of those two epic Cup ties played in January 1958. First we sensationally beat Arsenal 3-1, at the County Ground. The Gunners included England stars Danny Clapton, Vic Groves and Jimmy Bloomfield, and Welsh Internationals Jack Kelsey and Dave Bowen. Bobby Tebbutt, Barry Hawkins and Ken Leek scored for us in front of 21,344, who went wild as we clinched victory.

We were then drawn at Liverpool in the next round, and three weeks later we ran out at Anfield in front of a crowd of 56,939. After a tremendous battling performance we lost 1-3, Barry Hawkings scoring our only goal. The score was 1-1 until the closing minutes, when the legendary Billy Liddell centred, and Ben Collins tragically headed through his own goal. The England winger Alan A'Court sealed our fate.

Maurice Marston

Playing Torquay in an away fixture, Cobblers were well on top of the game, and we in defence pushed up to the half way line, to catch a long clearance by a Torquay defender. As I turned to chase I heard a whistle, so I continued running to retrieve the ball from outside the penalty area. In my haste I picked it up to throw it back up field. At that moment everyone shouted at once. It was not the referee who had blown the whistle, but a spectator. Torquay were awarded a free kick just outside the area which thankfully came to nothing. The manager's after-match comment was unprintable!

Ken Leek

When I first came to Northampton they had three teams, and I found myself in the third, which at the time competed in the UCL.

No sooner had I made the first team than I was called up; however, on my return I found myself making regular first team outings, and will never forget scoring the third goal against Arsenal in the FA Cup match, making the game safe.

I also recall my benefit match, which I shared with Roly Mills. By the time the game was played, I had joined Leicester City.

On my return to the Cobblers I recall netting against Southampton within three minutes of the match, in a great game that ended 2-2, when Bryan Harvey saved two penalties.

Another memory is scoring one of the two goals against West Ham in 1965 that gave us our first First Division victory.

Dave Bowen

The were many occasions when I was proud and privileged to be manager of Northampton Town FC — the day at Bury when we won promotion to the First Division was very memorable for me.

The journey from Division Four with little cash to spend was hard and difficult, but the positive attitude of all concerned, particularly Theo Foley and the players, made the near impossible task of promotion.

The second match that comes to mind, and which gave me great pleasure, was the match v Sunderland in Division Two, where conditions were very icy. I spent hours previous to the game experimenting with different forms of footwork, to combat the ice and snow that lay on the surface of the County Ground. After much deliberation, I decided that all our players should wear a ribbed soled canvas basketball boot, which I felt was perfect for the occasion.

The boots that day made us sure-footed, and we destroyed Sunderland 5-0, and I could not have been more pleased if I had scored a hat-trick.

Terry Branston

My debut at Peterborough, when we were 3-0 up at half time, in front of nearly 23,000, was very special. The support was great and they came back to draw 3-3.

Tommy Fowler was a legend at Northampton and I can remember having to mark him in practice matches; it certainly gave me the right grooming for my pro career.

At the same time Barry Lines joined the Club, and it was a delight to watch him mesmerise the full backs with his wonderful attacking play; I was surprised he was never snapped up by a First Division club.

The champion winning side of 1962/63 was special, with Chic Brodie in goal and a defence of Theo Foley, Mike Everitt, John Kurila — a match for any team.

John Reid, with a magic left foot and the heart of a Rolls Royce, dominated midfield, with the long legs of Derek Leck his perfect partner. Up front, Frank Large and Alex Ashworth scored the goals supplied by Billy Hails, Ray Smith and Barry Lines.

One of the most outstanding matches I can remember was in the '63-64 season, when we beat the pride of the north-east, Sunderland, 2-0 in front of a capacity crowd, away from home. Joe Kiernan skippered the side that day, and in the Sunderland side was the great Charlie Hurley.

The 1964-65 season saw us gain promotion to the First Division; Bryan Harvey made some outstanding penalty saves and played a major part in our promotion drive.

When I suffered a cartilage injury at Norwich I was unable to play again that season, and Graham Carr took my place and assured promotion with some sterling performances. At the heart of the Cobblers' defence, he had to wait a long time for his chance, and when it came, he took it with both hands. It's so nice to see old players doing well — Theo Foley at Arsenal, an outstanding captain in his day; Graham Carr, who has done a marvellous job since returning to Northampton, and his right hand man, Clive Walker; Joe Kiernan, the youth team coach, who gave all his skills to Northampton in his promotion year, and Mr 'Northampton', Roly Mills, who has done every job possible for the club — player, trainer, scout, ticket office and back room staff; 'Well done Bomber!'.

Theo Foley

My days at Northampton were the best of my playing career. I joined in 1961 from Exeter City. The Club had just been promoted to Division Three and I was joining a new team with plenty of good players, and then we made one of the best-ever signings, Cliff Holton from Watford. He scored 39 goals that season, and the following season we were promoted to Division Two; that was the best Third Division team the people of Northampton will ever see.

It was a more hard-working team we had in Division Two. I well remember that 4-1 win at Bury that gave us promotion to the First Division.

My fondest memory is of playing Everton at Goodison Park in the opening game of our First Division campaign; we lost, but the thrill of playing in the First Division for the Cobblers stands out. One day I hope to see them back there again. That day at Goodison I will never forget. There were many good players at the Club, but if I had to choose one out of the pack I would say John Reid.

Cliff Holton

My most memorable game for Northampton was my first. There was great secrecy involved, as Watford insisted on telling their fans I was not for sale. The local press suspected something, and followed me to work that morning, stayed watching my factory office. Later, Dave Bowen phoned and said he had clearance to sign me, and would I play that evening at Crystal Palace? I escaped from the factory and met the team at a Harrow hotel and duly signed on.

Later, as we were about to go out on the field, Dave Bowen threw me the ball and said, 'You're in charge on the field' (Such confidence).

History showed we won 4-1, and I got a hat-trick by courtesy of some great players who made up the team. With a start like that, and having such super players around me, breaking the Club's scoring record was made easy for me.

Frank Large

The first I knew about moving to the Cobblers was in the bad winter of 1963; I was with Queens Park Rangers at the time, and they had just moved to the White City for a trial period. I sat in the stand and watched them play Northampton, who were parading their new centre forward, Bert Llewellyn . However, he was carried off after only a few minutes' play, and within the week I was on my way to Northampton.

I used to travel up from London on a Friday night and I stopped with Graham Carr and Vic Cockcroft opposite the Black Lion public house in Marefair.

I just could not stop scoring, and that season we were promoted as Division Three champions. There was always a warm reception for me from the Northampton public. I can just remember the last match at home, when we received the Third Division championship trophy; I got concussed and don't remember much about it, except riding on an open topped 'bus through the streets.

What I enjoyed most at Northampton was the warm and friendly spirit at the Club, and the rapport we had with the supporters. On Tuesday evenings we would play different local teams at darts and skittles, and it was a great feeling to be involved.

The Cup match v Manchester United will always be in my memory; to be on the same pitch as Bobby Charlton and George Best, made it a wonderful day.

Don Martin

A couple of things stand out in my mind: the last game of the 1964-65 season, when we had won promotion to the First Division, was against Portsmouth, who in turn needed to draw to stay in the Second Division. The result was 1-1, and it was Jimmy Dickenson's last game; I remember we clapped him onto the pitch. After the game, the crowd stayed behind, and we all went up to the directors' box and threw our shirts to the crowd below; it was a fantastic feeling.

I well remember the four goals I scored v Brighton in the League Cup; also my first season back at Northampton, when I returned from Blackburn. We won promotion to the Third Division, under Bill Dodgin.

Joe Kiernan

My first memory at Northampton was in my third game. It was away to my old club, Sunderland. I was made captain for the day and, in front of 45,000 people, including my mother and father, the Cobblers won 2-0. The following season we won promotion to the First Division and it was achieved after a 4-1 win away at Bury; we did not realise it until after the game, when we heard the other results.

Playing in the First Division was a great experience, especially as I was the only ever-present that season, and I captained the side in Theo's absence. The home defeat by Fulham, which was really the game that saw us relegated, was a great disappointment. We were 2-1 up when George Hudson scored a fine goal; however, the 'keeper pulled the ball back over the line. I was standing only a few feet away and appealed to the referee, but he was not in a good position and in turn looked at the linesman, who had slipped and was also in no position to see. By this time the ball was back down the field, and I always felt that linesman's slip put us down.

With respect to the Second Division clubs, after Old Trafford, Anfield and White Hart Lane, it was a bit of an anti-climax.

The Manchester United cup-tie in 1970 was a disappointment, but I felt we should have had another penalty just after the one we were awarded; however, we did not, and failed to capitalise on the one we were given, hence we beat ourselves to a point. Had we taken a 2-0 lead, the score could have been different.

Of the players I played with, I must mention Theo Foley as the greatest skipper we ever had; even a 50% fit Theo was worth having on the field, just for his leadership qualities and, as for the most skillful, my old midfield team-mate, Graham Moore.

Tommy Robson

Being involved in Northampton's magnificent rise from the Fourth to the First Division, in just four years, is one happy memory of my time at the County Ground. There were all of those end-of-season promotion battles, and the crowd played their part in the Club's success story.

I've always had a soft spot for the Club, as they gave me my League break; I was an apprentice there at the same time as Graham Carr. There was always a great atmosphere at the Club and success followed success.

No particular game stands out for me, but I do remember once being knocked cold by the Norwich goalkeeper, Kevin Keelan, who was sent off in the process.

It was a thrill to play in the First Division, even though I only played seven matches before my £30,000 transfer to Chelsea.

Graham Carr

Probably my greatest moment as a player was gaining promotion from Division Two; I remember the game — it was at Bury on Easter Saturday and we won 4-1. As a manager it was winning the Fourth Division championship and winning the Fourth Division manager-of-the-season award at the same time.

Roger Barron

It was every local boy's dream to play for the home town club, so it was a great thrill when I signed professional terms for Northampton on my 18th birthday, especially as the Club had just been promoted to the First Division. At the time it had a staff of about 25 players, including two other goalkeepers.

There was Bryan Harvey, whose outstanding goalkeeping had helped to get the Cobblers into the First Division, and the long-serving Norman Coe, whom I used to watch as a schoolboy a few years earlier in the Fourth Division.

Although I did not make my first team debut until the end of season tour of Germany, it was still a memorable time to be at the club. I can still remember the trouble-free atmosphere created by crowds of 20,000, and reserve games often pulled in 5,000.

Clive Walker

I have many wonderful memories of my time at the County Ground too numerous to mention all. My most memorable moments as coach were obviously last season, when we won the Fourth Division championship.

As manager, the second round of the FA Cup in 1982/83 when we drew 1-1 at Gillingham; we then went on to win 3-2 and reached the third round of the FA Cup playing Aston Villa at home, when unfortunately we lost 0-1. Also as manager, the second round of the League Cup in 1979/80, which we won 3-0 against Oldham.

As a player, the most memorable game was the League Cup match in 1966/67, which we won 8-0 v Brighton.

Graham Felton

After spending nine years at the County Ground I obviously have several vivid memories. I was just 17-years-old when I signed for Northampton in September 1966, and imagine my amazement when I was selected to play in the first team, after a handful of reserve games. It was against Brighton on a Tuesday night, in the League Cup.

On the day of the match my excitement was coupled with terrible nerves, as I arrived for the game. However, we went on to win 8-0, and Don Martin scored four goals that night, and I felt I was walking on air, unable to sleep reliving the game over and over again. The same team was selected to travel to Ipswich for the Division Two match; this time I was on the wrong side of the thrashing, as we lost 6-1. In the space of a few days, at such a young age, I found out the meaning of the saying 'The ups and downs' of football — a hard lesson at the time.

A game that always springs to mind, when you talk to anyone of my era, is the Manchester United game, when we lost 2-8. My memory of that day is the players meeting before the match at the Whetstone hotel, where we were all given steaks (a rarity and a change from the usual egg on toast at a cafe). We arrived by 'bus at the County Ground, Abington was buzzing with activity and the adrenalin was flowing.

We ran out to a cheer of well over 20,000 — unheard of at the County ground — the atmosphere was electric. We lined up for the kick-off and I stood next to my hero, George Best, who had just returned from a six week suspension. I looked around: Bobby Charlton, Pat Crerand, these were all household names you read about. I was so much in awe of the occasion.

George Best scored six goals but, to see his unbelievable skill and ability was a privilege. Although the score suggests a whitewash, we put up a brave fight; I do not think I will, or can forget that day.

John Clarke
During my period at the Cobblers, I played under five managers, of whom two, Dave Bowen and Bill Dodgin, proved to be the most successful of recent times. Bowen was a great motivator, while Dodgin was a footballing perfectionist.

Obviously the one game that comes to mind was the 2-8 defeat by Manchester United in the FA Cup. George Best netted six goals after returning from a six week suspension, truly brilliant; my claim to fame in this game was that I laid on the second goal.

The season I remember most was 1970/71, when we had a truly good back four: Fairfax, Clarke, Rankmore, and Brookes; unfortunately we just missed out on promotion, owing to a serious injury to captain, Frank Rankmore, near the end of the season.

My sincere thanks go to the County Ground crowd who supported me well; this was shown when they kindly turned out for me in my testimonial match, arranged by Bill Dodgin v Leicester City in 1976. I trust and hope that many more local players will pull on the claret and white shirt, and enjoy the privilege, just as I did.

Phil Neal
I remember my early days at Northampton, working with groundsman Tom Harris, and I can remember working at the ground one summer and watching Colin Milburn knocking the West Indies for six, over on the cricket ground. I recall learning to drive in the Club's truck and, as an apprentice, one of my jobs was to take the socks out of the drier, knocking them against the wall to soften them up.

One day while cleaning the terraces I found a ten shilling note (50p), and all the apprentices had fish and chips for lunch. We had a big table in the dressing rooms and we would sling a net across it and play table tennis. Roly Mills would always beat the lads as he had the habit of looking one way and hitting the ball the other.

I can remember scoring eight goals in nine games, and then spending the rest of the season in defence. I sometimes wondered if playing in every position was doing my future any good; however it proved so in the end.

I have also had my share of disappointments, like scoring a late equaliser against Exeter in the FA Cup; when I came on as substitute but failed to make the team for the fifth round tie v Manchester United, though unknown to me at the time I would get the chance to play against United again, this time in the Cup-final, for Liverpool. Of the players I most admired at Northampton, I think Joe Kiernan and Billy Best stand out.

Paul Stratford
My favourite time at Northampton was during Bill Dodgin's reign as manager. There were some great characters at the Club during Bill's period, young and old; apart from a few sprints all training was mainly ball work, with Bill himself trying to prove he still had it when we finished training with five-a-side games.

We played a lot of attacking football at the time and I think the Sunday games brought the best out of us, and drew the crowds. One place we all feared to tread was McCormick's treatment room, and my experience in there still haunts me. When Dodgin left, after winning us promotion, I'm afraid the atmosphere changed in the dressing room, and it showed in the performances. However, the Liverpool game was a great consolation (Bowen's testimonial), and that, along with playing alongside the lads, is an experience I will always cherish.

Billy Best

Having been at the Club for ten years, I have several memorable moments. I made my debut in the first team v Norwich City and scored a goal, which I suppose is the best moment I can remember.

I was also in the first team when we won our first ever First Division game v West Ham United.

When I came back to Northampton for my second spell, I was lucky enough to play under Bill Dodgin, a very good manager. This was the best period. He got us promotion to the Third Division, and being captain of the side is something to remember; also the fact that I played, and scored, in all four Divisions of the League for the same Club — an achievement I am proud of.

Dixie McNeil

During my playing career, I was lucky enough to attain promotion twice, once with Hereford and once with Wrexham. However, as a young lad, I had visions of promotion with Northampton in my second season there. That was until that dreaded man, George Best, came along to the County Ground with his Manchester United team and beat us 8-2 in the FA Cup. I remember that week well, for we trained believing the danger would be Bobby Charlton. Cut him out and we had a chance. However, 'Besty' showed his mercurial skills, and proceeded to score six goals on his own. Every now and again it is still rubbed in when they show it on TV. No doubt Frank Large, like myself, wonders why our goal apiece isn't shown as well. Still, what a memory to score against Manchester United.

Stuart Robertson

I enjoyed the whole time I spent playing for the Cobblers and I have nothing but fond memories, helped especially with the rapport I enjoyed with the supporters.

Two particular highlights were the promotion-winning season, and the great cameraderie of the team, plus my winning the supporters' Player-of-the-year award.

One amusing incident took place at Colchester, when I was 'taken short' during the second half, and asked the referee's permission to leave the field. This took him completely by surprise, as he said he had never encountered the problem before.

I returned some four to five minutes later, much to the amusement of the crowd, to immediately score with a header from a corner. I am sure the fact that I had lost two to three pounds enabled me to jump higher to reach the ball!

Keith Williams

I remember a man who was very much a part of Northampton Town Football Club, and who helped me immensely when I was unfortunate enough to pick up a serious injury. His name was Mac 'the thumbs' McCormick, and he had the biggest pair of thumbs I had ever seen, and my, did he put them to good use. But it was sheer agony at the time, and the language that came out of that treatment room, when Mac got to work, was something else. People walking down the street must have thought we were being tortured, not treated. But he would get you fit, and that was his job. Mac made my stay at Northampton very enjoyable, but then so did a lot of people, and I'll take this opportunity of thanking the supporters of Northampton for making my stay a happy and enjoyable experience.

George Reilly

I am reminded of Northampton Town FC every morning, when I look in the mirror and see my 'beautiful face' — I am minus two front teeth, elbowed out by a belligerent Bradford City centre half in an away game, on one cold winter evening, when I was a fresh-faced nineteen-year-old, back in 1977.

That day I was wearing the number nine shirt; it was a miserable day all round, and we lost 3-1. I could tell the referee had no sympathy for me when he accused me of trying to bite the centre half's elbow!

On a serious note, I look back on my old days with Northampton with affection and still look with interest for their results.

John Buchanan

I have some fond memories of Northampton Town; I signed for them at the age of 18, for the grand sum of 22 shillings a week (£1 10), and a big difference of 11 pence (5p) from what I was earning as an apprentice electrician. Players such as Large, McNeil, Fairbrother, Clarke, Kiernan, Rankmore and Neal were in the team at the time and I looked up to them.

I remember being substitute in a game v Scunthorpe, with Kevin Keegan sitting on the other substitute's bench; I got on for about five minutes, which was pleasing, as the bonus was £5 per point.

It took around 16 months for me to settle, coming from the Highlands; I remember around Christmas time I was put into hospital because I had a breathing problem. I had my nose broken and reset, and I was hardly out a couple of days before 'Mac' had me doing laps of the ground, and I passed out. That was Charlie, like me a Scotsman; believe me we had some battles, but always ended up the best of friends. I also have great respect for Dave Bowen, who signed me and was a great manager with both Northampton and Wales.

I have always got on well with the supporters, but not so much with referees; maybe it was my Scots temper!

I scored a lot of goals for the Club, and I remember them all; I believe I was the first player to score on a Sunday for Northampton, and I think it was against Rotherham when we won 2-1, with myself netting both goals. The two greatest goals I scored were on a Wednesday night when we went to Reading. They were top of the League, and we were struggling for points; we won 2-1 and I netted both goals, from 25 yards, one with the left foot and one with the right, neither more than a foot off the ground.

The apprentices stayed with Mr and Mrs Graves at the Club hostel in Park Avenue North, along with the professionals who lived far from home. I have a lot of fond memories with the younger players like Barry Tucker, John Gregory, Ken Parker, Peter Hawkins, Alan Oman and Dave Bukowski.

I met a girl from Boughton and got married, and that helped me to settle; Barry Tucker and I both got married on the same day. I still try to see the boys when I come to Northampton.

Phil Neal joined Liverpool about the same time that I moved to Cardiff, and it's nice to see him and John Gregory do so well.

Steve Massey

One match sticks in my mind more than any other for sheer excitement, a nail-biting finale, and my best goal for Northampton.

Drawn away to Gillingham in the second round of the FA Cup, when they were top of Division Three, we were given no chance. We pulled off a shock and held them to a 1-1 draw. The draw for the third round was made and it was a home tie against the holders of the European Cup, Aston Villa. What an incentive!

The replay attracted over 4,000, twice the average crowd — could we pull it off?

The score was 1-1, and extra time looming when, in the last seven unbelievable minutes the crowd witnessed first joy, as Frankie Belfon scored his second, 2-1, then stunned silence as Gillingham equalised straight away, then ultimately frenzied relief as I scored my best goal for the Cobblers just two minutes from time. I turned on the edge of the box, and curled a left footer over the 'keeper and into the net. 'Bring on Villa!' We had done it.

Wakely Gage

Almost every season I played at Northampton was spent battling against relegation; we failed only twice. During this period the only constant factor was the coming and going of numerous players, and of managers every season.

Several times we would have long spells without winning, and the directors would come up with an idea to lift everyone's spirits. On a Friday morning after training, all the players would be ordered into the directors' lounge, where we would find a small buffet, bottles of sherry and cans of beer. A couple of directors would then join us and we would get stuck into the food and drink.

As far as I can remember, every time we had one of these parties, we would win the following Saturday. It was always joked about: we should do it every week, although we never did. Perhaps if we had we would have won promotion.

Alec Smith (Chairman of the Northampton Town Football Supporters' Club)

Alec, married to Evelyn, has two sons and a

daughter. Evelyn can be seen at home matches, selling programmes outside the main stand and around the ground (the only lady seller). Oldest son, Alan, is a steward, and younger son, John, is a special constable; both are on duty most home match days.

On leaving the Army, Alec joined Kettering Town Supporters' Club and was the assistant secretary; he was with the Club for 18 years until he moved to Northampton. In 1967, both he and Evelyn joined the Northampton Town Supporters' Club, Alec being invited onto the committee in 1975, and Evelyn in November of the same year.

Both are members of the mounties and steward on one of the coaches for away matches. In 1981 Alec was elected vice chairman. Two years later Evelyn became secretary and in 1983 Alec took over as chairman.

As affiliated members of the National Federation of Football Supporters' Clubs, both have represented Northampton at these meetings, and did so recently at Brighton to celebrate 60 years' membership (Northampton were founder members).

Evelyn is now assistant secretary, but both are still heavily involved and the motto is 'To help, not to hinder'.

1962-63 team. (C&E)

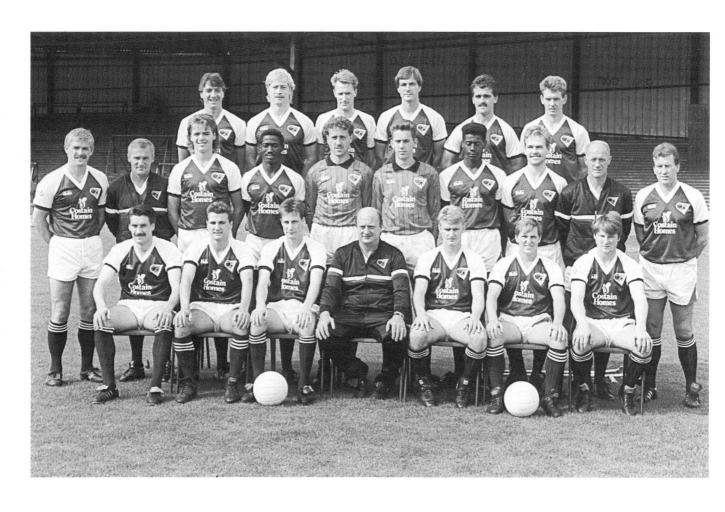

Team 1988/89 — back row: P. Culpin, G. Reed, T. Adcock, T. Slack, E. McGoldrick, P. Wilson; middle row: J. Holmes (youth team coach), D. Casey (Physio.), I. Johnston, K. McPherson, P. Gleasure, G. Sylvester, G. Donegal, R. Wilcox, C. Walker (Coach), B. Knight (Reserve team coach); front row: D. Thomas, D. Longhurst, B. Sanderman, G. Carr (Manager), M. Singleton, D. Gilbert, W. Donald. (C&E)

THE CURRENT SQUAD

ADCOCK, Anthony Charles (Adi)   Forward
Born in Bethnal Green on 27 March 1963, he started his career with Colchester United and made his debut in May 1981, as an 18-year-old. In six seasons at Layer Road, he scored 112 goals and, despite offers from Germany, he decided to move to Manchester City for £85,000. Although it was a short stay, just six months, he netted nine goals, including two hat-tricks in five days, v Huddersfield and Plymouth. January 1988 saw him join Northampton as part of the deal that took Trevor Morley to Manchester City, and he paid back part of his £75,000 fee in his second game, when he scored a late equaliser v Wigan.

BUNCE, Paul   Midfield
Born Coalville 7 January 1967, he started his career with Leicester City but was restricted to seven outings. When promotion was assured from the Fourth Division, Cobblers manager Graham Carr bought him to Northampton for £5,000; although not a regular in the side, he has netted twice for the Club.

CHARD, Phillip John   Utility
Corby born (16 October 1960), Phil started his career with Notts Forest, but failed to break into their first team, hence he joined Peterborough, making his debut for them in April 1979. He asked for a move in 1985, which coincided with manager Graham Carr's building programme and he thought nothing of paying £11,000 for him.

Since then Phil has played in every outfield position and, when Trevor Morley left, he was made captain. On Sundays he takes charge of the youth team.

COY, Robert   Defender
Born in Birmingham on 30 November 1961, Bob started his career with Wolves, leaving them for Chester in 1983. Two seasons there and voted player-of-the-year, he was released. At the start of the 1986 season he joined the Cobblers (on trial), as regular central defender Russell Wilcox injured himself in the pre-season tour. After a handful of games he was offered full terms and held his place until Russell regained full fitness; since then he has not been a regular in the side, but has helped out both Aylesbury and Altrincham.

CULPIN, Paul   Forward
Born Kirby Muxloe (8 February 1963) and unable to find a way through the Leicester first team, he dropped into non-League football with Nuneaton, while Graham Carr was the manager there, and became a consistent scorer. When Graham joined Northampton, Paul was one of his first targets; however the striker decided on a move to Coventry for £50,000. Two and a half seasons realised only 11 appearances and two goals so, when Graham approached him again, it was £55,000 that changed hands and Paul became a Cobbler. A great run of six goals in five games, plus two more v Watford in Clive Walker's testimonial came to an end with an injury that has sidelined him for some time.

DONALD, Warren (Wazzer)   Midfield
Uxbridge-born (7 October 1964) Warren first came to Northampton on loan from West Ham in March 1985, while Tony Barton was manager. He so impressed Graham Carr when he took over that he put in an offer for the ex-England schoolboy international, of £11,000, and purchased the tenacious midfielder. He is one of the hardest shots at the County Ground.

DONEGAL, Glenville   Forward
He won his first outing last season in the FA Cup match v Southend and opened his account last season with a fine goal v Ipswich in the League Cup. A tall player, who once he masters first team football will be a great asset; supporters still remember his later equaliser v Walsall when he came on as substitute.

GILBERT, David James   Midfielder
Lincoln was his birthplace on 22 June 1963, and his first Club, where he set a record of 15 substitute appearances in a season. A short stay at Scunthorpe was followed by a drop into non-League football with Boston, where Graham ressurrected his League career by, not only bringing him to Northampton, but putting him straight into the first team. Here he settled down to an attacking midfield role, and took over the added responsibility of penalty taker, already holding the Club record for the most conversions.

GLEASURE, Peter Francis   Goalkeeper
Born Luton 8 October 1960, he joined Millwall and was a member of their youth cup-winning side. He soon broke into the first team but, when he lost his place, he agreed to join Northampton on loan in March 1983. At the end of the season he signed full terms, hence he became the longest serving player. In all his time here he has missed only five games, each one because a cover 'keeper was tried out.

HARRIS, Alan   Goalkeeper
Nuneaton born (13 March 1969), Alan played for the Midland club before joining Northampton in a £15,000 deal with Eddie McGoldrick. Although not yet a first teamer, Alan gave a sterling display for Luton when he guested for them in a testimonial match at the County Ground.

LOGAN, David   Defender
Whitley born (5 December 1963), he started his career with Doncaster, joining Northampton in February 1987 for £20,000, to fill a problem left back spot.

LONGHURST, David   Forward
Born in Corby (15 Janaury 1965) David was another Forest apprentice, but stayed in League football with Halifax. Graham Carr made several attempts to buy him, achieving so in the close season of 1987 for £40,000, which at the time equalled the record fee.

McGOLDRICK,
   Eddie John Paul   Midfield/winger
Born in London 30 April 1965, Eddie was part of the deal that brought him and Alan Harris here in 1986. A match winger on his day, Eddie has been on the books of Peterborough, Nuneaton and Kettering Town. At the height of the Club's fame last season, Eddie, who was born of Irish parentage, was being earmarked for an Eire cap.

McPHERSON,
   Keith Anthony (Macca)   Defender
Yet another Londoner (11 September 1963), Keith's first claim to fame was to be a member of the West Ham youth team that won the Youth Cup in 1981. His one and only appearance for West Ham was in May 1985 v Liverpool. He first joined Cambridge United on loan in 1985 and later, when Gavin Nebbelling returned to Crystal Palace, he joined the Cobblers. Since that day in January 1986 he has been a regular member of the side; as well as a first-class defender, his aerial power in the box has seen his name on the scoresheet more than once.

REED, Graham (Rambo)   Defender
Doncaster born 24 June 1961, Graham started as a striker with Barnsley but was released after a season. He stepped into non-League football with Frickley, and it was from here that Graham made him a League footballer again. Again he was bought as a striker, and scored in his Cobblers debut v Burnley but, during an injury crisis, he was reverted to defender and has stayed there ever since.

SINGLETON, Martin   Midfield
Banbury born (2 August 1963), Martin was a former England Youth International and started his career at Coventry, scoring on his debut v Everton in April 1983. In 1985 he joined Bradford City, helping them to the Second Division, and he was in the side that saw the horrific fire. The following season he became a West Brom player and stayed two seasons, before breaking the Cobblers' record fee and coming to Northampton for £57,000.

SLACK, Trevor   Defender
Born Peterborough 26 September 1962, he played well over 200 games for the 'Posh' and was well known at Northampton, making some 14 appearances against the Cobblers over the years.

100

He was one of manager Graham Carr's first targets while a Peterborough player, but the asking price was too high.

Since then he has had spells at Rotherham and Grimsby, before coming to Northampton for £10,000 in February 1988.

WILCOX, Russell (Ronnie)   Defender
Born Hemsworth 25 May 1964, Doncaster was Russell's first club but, after only one appearance, he dropped into non-League football and enjoyed it so much he won England semi-professional caps, and became Frickley's player-of-the-year.

His Cobblers' debut was postponed when he was injured during the pre-season; however, when he won back his place in September 1986, he became a regular in the side.

WILSON, Paul   Defender
Born in Bradford on 2 April 1968, he started with Huddersfield Town, where he made nine appearances before joining Norwich. Being unable to break into the first team, he agreed to join Northampton on loan, to fill a left back spot that had been a problem for the manager since he arrived in 1985.

Warren Donald slides the ball away from Torquay's Russell Musker.
(PN)

Russell Wilcox, Northampton's centre half, in an aerial tussle with Phil
Sproson of Port Vale. (C&E)

UPDATE 1985-87

1985/86: 'It is always darkest before the dawn', and so it proved to be for Northampton Town, as their recent history unfolded like a script for a *Boys Own* story.

As the '84/85 season drew to a close, the Club was having one of its worse seasons ever, both on and off the field. As if sitting bottom of the Fourth Division was not enough, the directors had put the Club up for sale; there were rumours of a merger with neighbours Kettering Town and support was at an all-time low. However, as in all good *Boys Own* stories, the hero or in this case heroes, came through.

Mike Conroy, a local brewery worker, was discussing the Club's plight with a long-time friend, Derek Banks, a Watford-based tobacco importer, and suggested that he might like to buy himself a football club. Meanwhile, in a Northampton snooker club, two local businessmen, Barry Stonhill and Charlie Barham, who were also two of the Cobblers' supporters, were also discussing the Club's plight, and between them and several business colleagues, a consortium was formed, labelling itself 'Friends of the Cobblers'.

From this platform, changes took place. Derek Banks became chairman, and two consortium members also joined the board — Charlie Barham and Mark Deane — although later on several more members of the consortium joined as well. Manager Tony Barton left the Club and his replacement was the supporters' choice, Graham Carr, the ex-Cobblers defender who had pulled Nuneaton from the Southern League to the Alliance Premier.

He allowed the same players to play out the remaining seven games of the '84/85 season and, under his inspiration, six were won, allowing the Club to overtake Torquay and keep a record of never having finished bottom of any division since joining the Football League.

Then, at the end of the season, it was a case of rolling up the sleeves and sorting out the Club. Graham Carr's first job was to find competent playing staff. Only six of the seventeen were retained, and the Club's new manager stepped back into the non-League to bring, first Trevor Morley and Richard Hill from Nuneaton, then Graham Reed, a miner from Frickley, and from the League, Paul Curtis from Charlton and Ian Dawes from Newcastle. With these and the remaining players from last season, he embarked on a pre-season tour of the north-east, something that would become a ritual in following seasons.

The opening game of the season was at Burnley. Strangely the last time Northampton went to Turf Moor for a League game, Graham Carr was a Cobblers' player, back in 1965.

It was no fairy tale start; at half-time it was 3-0 to the Lancashire team, but Morley and Reed did open their accounts for the Club in the second half, bringing the score to a more respectable 3-2.

It proved to be just a hiccough as the side settled down to some fine victories, including a 6-0 win over Preston. The buying hadn't stopped. Phil Chard was signed from Peterborough in time for him to play against his old club, and Warren Donald, another midfield player, was bought from West Ham, after spending part of the previous season on loan to Northampton.

Although Russell Lewis was playing well in the heart of the defence, it was a problem finding a centre back partner; first Ian Dawes was tried, then Graham Reed was moved back, then Gavin Nebbelling was signed on loan from Crystal Palace, but the end asking price was above the manager's value, so he was replaced by Keith McPherson from the West Ham school; he later signed full terms.

After the disaster of the previous season, there was talk of promotion; suddenly the Club was scoring goals, five at Peterborough and Cambridge, then five against Torquay. Benjamin, Hill and Morley were all finding the net. Unfortunately it was a run-in that the Club failed to capitalise. In the last eight games, only six points were collected. Had maximum points been attained, then so would promotion. However, things were on the up and up, and in his first full season, Graham Carr had put together an exciting team. Support began to grow, and Northampton were no longer a joke.

Off the field, Derek Banks and his team were also hard at work. Sponsorship had been sought, and every effort was being made to make the ground as safe and comfortable as possible.

In fact the ground was the biggest bone of contention. The police and fire brigade had made many demands on the Club. The old wooden stand was dismantled and small portable ones assembled around the ground. They closed off part of the Spion Kop, asking for observation points to be built for the police.

Whatever was spent on the ground, and it ran into thousands of pounds, was dead money, as the ground was not the Club's. There was no way they would ever see a return, but it was a case of one step at a time.

1986/87: only a few new faces appeared for this season: Eddie McGoldrick, a winger, and Alan Harris, a goalkeeper, were bought from Nuneaton for a combined fee of £15,000, while Dave Gilbert, once rejected by both Lincoln and Scunthorpe, returned to League action via Boston. Russell Wilcox, a central defender, came from Frickley to replace Russell Lewis, who in turn had joined Kettering town. But problems arose before the season started; Wilcox was injured pre-season, so Bob Coy was signed from Chester as cover.

A 2-0 lead at Scunthorpe was dropped, and both clubs left the field with a point each. It was not until the fourth game of the season that people began to sit up. A 2-1 victory over Peterborough saw the Club top of the Fourth Division for the first time since the 1975/76 season. Ironically, Northampton was to suffer just one defeat in the following 23 League games, and that was at Swansea.

The FA Cup also brought its share of excitement, as well as disappointment. The first hurdle was easily cleared: a 3-0 victory over local rivals Peterborough, the first time we had ever done the treble over them, was followed by a thirteen-goal, two-match thriller against promotion bedmates, Southend. The first game at Roots Hall ended 4-4, and it seemed they would clinch the replay by taking a 2-1 half-time lead. However, the referee went off injured, and his replacement gave the Cobblers two penalties, which Dave Gilbert obliged by converting both.

Round three was a plum away tie, at Newcastle, and special weekends were arranged for supporters to travel to the game. The town was buzzing, and the media began

to build the game up. However, it turned sour when the game was postponed through bad weather and, when it was at last played, after only a few minutes skipper Trevor Morley was carried off and, if that was not bad enough, the Cobblers conceded an early goal. Top scorer Richard Hill gave the side hope with an equaliser but, in a goalmouth scramble, the Magpies won the tie.

The championship was achieved in the 43rd League game and the last home game, when Crewe was beaten 2-1. The players showed their appreciation of the supporters by throwing their shirts into the crowd at the end of the game.

The championship was assured, and Graham Carr voted Division Four Manager-of-the-month. Richard Hill joined Watford for over £250,000 — a great end to the season. A fantastic end-of-season open-topped 'bus ride for the players from the County ground, to the Town hall preceded a civic reception, overwhelmingly supported by the people of Northampton, who turned out in thousands along the town streets, waving banners and scarves, babies in Cobblers colours, chi ours, with photos of their heroes, a sight that many older supporters thought they would never see again after the dizzy heights of the '60s.

In the '87/88 season the Club made a strong challenge for further promotion to the Second Division but, in the final run-in, due to illness and injuries, they failed to make the play-offs — by a mere two points. But Graham Carr's side had now consolidated and, in no way discouraged for this was early days, looked forward to the new season with their confidence undiminished.

In latter years this period of the Club's history will be looked upon as a re-birth, proving that enthusiasm, the right backing and a little money enables clubs to go from strength to strength. The final piece of the jigsaw is missing . . . a new ground. With a new home, new doors open the sky becomes the limit; without it Northampton Town could become another of those names left to gather dust in the archives of the Football League, like Accrington Stanley or Bradford Park Avenue.

The decision lies with the people of Northampton . . . every click of the turnstiles is a breath of life for the Club.

104

Trevor Morley is sandwiched between Andy Beesley and Jeff Doyle of Peterborough; looking on, Northampton's Richard Hill, and Peterborough's ex-Cobbler's defender, Wakeley Gage. (PN)

ABOVE: Dave Gilbert averts a sliding tackle from Southend's Paul Roberts, Paul Culpin looks on in the background. (PN) BELOW: Trevor Morley takes a tumble in the home match v Cardiff in the 1986/87 season. (PN)

106

INDEX

110

SUBSCRIBERS

PRESENTATION COPIES

1 **Northampton Town Football Club**
2 **Northampton Borough Council**
3 *Chronicle & Echo*
4 **Derek Banks**
5 **Graham Carr**
6 **Russell Wilcox**

7 Frank Grande
8 John Harley
9 Clive & Carolyn Birch
10 N.C. Skedge
11 Mrs B. Amos
12 John White
13 Gary Mabee
14 Tim Franks
15 D.E. Bell
16 P. Collins
17 Mrs Evelyn Smith
18 John Lucas
19 J.R. Ellard
20 Gary Lewis
21 M.J. Spooner
22 Richan Booth
23 Julie Attwell
24 Jan Buitenga
25 M. Berry
26 L.J. Hawkins
27 Malcolm Mullally
28 Mrs Balhatchet
29 T. Foley
30 Robin Smith
31 Peter Isham
32 Carl Isham
33 Don Welch
34 Ian Welch
35 Phil Abel
36 Mrs M.F. Routhorn
37 Leslie Pendered
38 A.W. Brown
39 Mrs B. Wood
40 R. Stevenson
41 Robin Marshall
42 R. Hinde
43 Roger Averill
44 P. Hobbins
45 P. Bowers
46 D. Little

47 Edward Redmond
48 Stephen Hollowell
49 Peter Tullett
50 Robert Swann
51 R.J. Carter
52 M.D. Hawkins
53 N.C. Skedge
54 William Rich
55 Keith Rich
56 Mark Bamford
57 Colin Eldred
58 C. Gammage
59 P.J. Warnes
60 K.J. Smith
61 John Staiger
62 Gary Merritt
63 Robert Cook
64 Renny Wadsworth
65 N.A. Maycock
66 Andy Farmer
67 Matthew Webb
68 Anne Gibbs
69 A.J.B. Harries
70 M.J. Dearden
71 Gary Spooner
72 A.H. Driver
73 M.R. Driver
74 N.A. Driver
75 Miss Jayne Hill
76 N.G. Birkert
77 G.J. Wilson
78 Scott Desborough
79 P.J. Desborough
80 D.F. Jones
81 Philip Palmer
82 N.J. Haycox
83 P.E. Nunley
84 David Nunley
85 D. Mead
86 R.J. Hamley

87 David Howe
88 Stephen Serbyn
89 R.L. Denny
90 Stephen Rodhouse
91 Terry Rodhouse
92 Graham Rodhouse
93 Mike Serbyn
94 J. Payne
95 C. Bailey
96 Andrew Little
97 R. Billingham
98 P.J. Austen
99 Brian John Coles
100 C.J. Davies
101 S.J. Newcombe
102 Peter Reynolds
103 Peter Allen
104 Sid Bull
105 G. Baxter
106 R.W. Jones
107
108 P. Blane
109 Amanda Scott
110 Ray Pitt
111 Martin Cave
112 Derek Burton
113 Geoff Welsh
114 Andy Robinson
115 Steven Manning
116 C.R. Cooper
117 Scott Desborough
118 Barry Blundell
119 Len Banks
120 Barry Stonhill
121 Grahame Wilson
122 Bob Church
123 Mark Deane
124 Eric Northover
125 Stuart Wilson
126 Dick Underwood

127 J.R. Allen
128 D.G. Church
129 Tony Bluff
130 Keith Lowe
131 Ian John Swain
132 Bob Kirk
133 P.K. Liddington
134 Gary Tucker
135 William Robert Humphrey
136 R.L. Farmer
137 Kevin Sykes
138 Daryl Read
139 Gordon Marriott
140 Kevin Wayne Johnson
141 Anthony Wilson
142 Eddie & Mary Bott
143 Russell Bott
144 Peter Eaton
145 Mr J.M. & Mrs
146 S.C. Clack
147 S.J. Bence
148 Sally Louise Knight
149 D.W. Pegg
150 Derek Chapman
151 Ian Grant
152 Neil Eaton
153 Andrew Roberts
154
155 David Folwell
156 A.J.B. Harris
157 Roy Marriott
158 Stephen R. Haynes
159 David Cockerill
160 Mrs Collyer
161 T.R. Green
162 Paul Judkins
163 Peter Nicholson
164 Mark Kirby

165 John Whiting	234 Graham Felton	291 Alan Clarke	348 Ivan Lack
166 Anthony J. Galsworthy	235 F.A.B. King	292 G.T. Allman	349 Alan Trudgill
167 A.R. Britten	236 T. Fowler	293 John Lathan	350 Jeff Trudgill
168	237 Keith R. Harrison	294 P.W. Stevenson	351 P.J. Laukatts
169 D.W. Thompson	238 John Maycock	295 W.D. Phillips	352 Roy Pope
170 Bill Craven	239 W.H. Wooding	296 Michael Braham	353 G. Robinson
171 Colin Rogers	240 Donald Adams	297 Simon Oliver	354 D. Robinson
172 C.R. Facer	241 Mark Brooksbank	298 Gordon Hadland	355 Mike Deacon
173 A.N. Foster	242 D. Toseland	299 J. Gardiner	356 Harry Deacon
174 John Ward	243 Andrew Ray Taylor	300 A.R. Platt	357 Alistair Brooker
175 Gerry Reilly	244 Mrs R. Mullings	301 Michael Campbell	358 N.H. Adams
176 Simon York	245 Nick Cockerill	302 M.J. O'Connor	359 P.R. Minney
177 John Searg	246 Stuart Robinson	303 Geir Juva	360 John Watson
178 Nigel Summers	247 Sally Lloyd Parry	304 Gareth M. Davies	361 Pete Smith
179 T.P. Barnes	248 Steven Alibone	305 Roy L. Pope	362 Keith Onley
180 Albert Powell	249 B.J. Spick	306 Stuart Beeson	363 Glen Powell
181 Martyn J. Dearden	250 Clive Richard Cox	307 Lars-Olof Wendler	364 Jim Powell
182 Dave Walden	251 Ben Collins	308 Wallace Brown	365 M.L. Hopkins
183 Mrs K. Clements	252	309 Vivian & Rita Long	366 Peter Cooke
184 Dustine Grande	253 Wakeley Gage	310 Peter Baxter	367 I.L. Cooper
185 Northampton Town Supporters' Club	254	311 M. Swart	368 J. Brunt
186 Northamptonshire County Library	255 Donnon Martin	312 Wade Martin	369 M.G. Jones
201	256 Edward Smith	313 K.M. Torgrimsen	370 Mike Taylor
202 Rev D. Abraham	257 John Harris	314 C.C. Hayes	371 I.F. Smith
203 I. Griffiths	258 Derek Hyde	315 William Donnachie	372 John Alun Griffiths
204 Tony Kingston	259 Peter Hutchins	316 Raymond J. Bailey	373 Jeff Warren
205 S. Corby	260 D. Walton	317 Dave Clarke	374 A.E. Marks
206 Sgt D. McCann	261 John Musgrove	318 James Lawson	375 J.A. Rabbitt
207 John Rawlings	262 L. A. Zammit	319 Duncan Watt	376 Martyn Peacock
208 David Hawkins	263 David Earnshaw	320 Terry Frost LCIOB	377 Dennis Barter
209 Michael Martin	264 John Treleven	321 Alan Hindley	378 L.W. Arnold
210 C.A. Canvin	265 Richard Wells	322 M.J. Candlin	379 Stephen Sharpley
211 John Whelan	266 David Sullivan	323 Karen Knight & Ian Naylor	380 F. Davis
212 Ian Davies	267 Steve Massey	324 Keith Bryan Ducker	381 Anthony Seas
213 Amanda Evans	268 Bryan Massey	325 Dafydd Williams	382 Roger Arthur Hickman
214 Russell John Cashmore	269 Gerald Hill	326 Martyn Baker	383 Barry Underwood
215 Alan Claridge	270 D.C. Wheatley	327 A.F.J. Rixon	384 Mr & Mrs R.J. Hefford
216 Peter Graham	271 Moira & Frederick Furness	328 Martin Harris	385 Gavin Jones
217 Stewart Farmer	272 Richard Stockem	329 D. Norris	386 David F. Allen
218 David Beer	273 Ian Watts	330 A. Mills	387 Andrew Wright
219 David Dickens	274 Steven Minney	331 Clive Reece	388 Terry McClure
220 Andrew Gregg	275 David Rush	332 L. Batch	389 S.R. Denton
221 S.D. Craxton	276 George Ernest Wiles	333 Gerald Pitt	390 Ann L. Whitworth
222 Peter Capell	277 Mike Purkiss	334 Tony Wright	391 W.J. Fitzhugh
223 Paul Gardham	278 Ian Griffiths	335 Desmond White	392 Stuart McClure
224 John Taylor	279 Dixie McNeil	336 A. Frampton	393 Peter Blunt
225 Colin Taylor	280 K.P. Wood	337 Ian Lightwood	394 Philip Breed
226 Neil Saunders	281 Colin Cameron	338 Graham Mann	395 Jack Mould
227 Dominic Lynskey	282 William Needs	339 Brian Webster	396 Roger Wiggins
228 P. Blake	283 David Keats	340 Mr Tack	397 Barrie Kirk
229 R. Sturgen	284 Norman Green	341 Mike Cox	398 Gary Twiselton
230 N.S. Davis	285 J.F. Burrell	342 I.L. Skeats	399 Patrick Kirk
231 B.E. Davis	286 Keith William Jones	343 R. Johnson	400 Michael William Newton
232 Stephen Rose	287 A.N. Davis	344 G. Pettifer	*Remaining names unlisted*
233 Stephen Byrne	288 A.K. Ambrosen	345 R.W. Kirk	
	289 David Downs	346 John Fisher	
	290 M. Featherstone	347 Darren Lack